The Potluck Blueprint

A call to fellowship through food and Scripture

By Lady Rhonda

The Potluck Blueprint
© 2016
VoicePenPurpose Publishing ™
Cover Design by James, GoOnWrite.com

Published December 2016
ISBN-10:0-9978394-2-2
ISBN-13:978-0-9978394-2-5

DISCLAIMER

Dedication

To my daddy for being a spiritual leader in my life.
To my loyal sisters, committed aunt, and my adorable daughters
for loving me unconditionally.
To my steadfast friends who relentlessly said I must write a
book. To the members of Saint John's CME Church, my family and
friends who donated the recipes featured in this book.
And, finally, in memory of my mother who instilled in me both
courage and strength.
I ask God how I can pray for you all.

**"For this reason, since the day we heard about you, we
have not stopped praying for you. We continually ask God
to fill you with the knowledge of his will through all the
wisdom and understanding that the Spirit gives, so that
you may live a life worthy of the Lord and please him in
every way: bearing fruit in every good work, growing in
the knowledge of God, being strengthened with all power
according to his glorious might so that you may have great
endurance and patience, and giving joyful thanks to the
Father, who has qualified you to share in the inheritance of
his holy people in the kingdom of light. For he has rescued
us from the dominion of darkness and brought us into the
kingdom of the Son he loves, in whom we have redemption,
the forgiveness of sins."**
Colossians 1:9-14

Table of Contents

Preface

Each morning I wake up with enthusiasm and a sense of gratitude. From the time I open my eyes until my feet touch my carpeted bedroom floor, I am consumed with awareness that my life has been blessed. My breath is even and steady, my body is strong and alert, and my mind is clear and focused. It is in this moment that I ask God how I can be of service to others. These days I open myself up to the direction God sets out before me and it has made all the difference in my happiness.

> *"In all thy ways acknowledge Him,*
> *and He shall direct thy paths."*
> *Proverbs 3:6*

From an outsider's perspective, I appear successful. From my decorated military career, beautiful triplet girls, and our spacious family homes, everything looks perfect. From an insider's point of view, my life has been riddled with tragedy after my mother's early death and two short-lived marriages; one ended through divorce and the other through widowhood. Neither perspective encompasses my faith, however, and that is where my true blessings lie.

Becoming a widow, in particular, has been a transformative experience. In my heart, nothing had prepared me for that moment. I couldn't stop saying to myself, "He was supposed to live." Now what do I do? I felt numb and adrift after receiving the news of his passing. Thankfully my sister drove me home from the hospital that fateful night. I remember sitting silently in the passenger seat. I had no words; I could only think about my daughters.

The God who is in his holy dwelling place is the father of the fatherless and the defender of widows.
Psalm 68:5

During that drive, I remembered losing my mother as a teenager. It broke my heart to think about my girls growing up without their father.

I assumed that this was the biggest test God had for me, but I was wrong. As I moved forward with burial arrangements, I learned that we didn't have enough insurance money to pay the mortgage off. Not only did we lose my husband and my children's father, but now the girls and I had to move out of our family home.

Within a week, I learned that our house was worth $200,000 less than what we owed on it. The banks didn't care that I had just lost my husband's income, had three young daughters, and no equity in the house. Even though I had not missed a mortgage payment and my credit was still strong, things would shift dramatically if I didn't take action soon. I knew if we stayed in that house longer than three years I would no longer be able to pay the mortgage at my current income.

I called out, "God, please hear my cry and help me now!"

There was silence.

"God you promised You would supply all my needs..."

Again, I waited for an answer.

Eventually I fell asleep as I remembered this passage:

> ***"But my God shall supply all your needs according to his riches in glory by Christ Jesus***
> ***Philippians 4:19***

Something changed that night; maybe it was my prayer being answered or my fear being swallowed up by faith. Either way, when I stopped worrying and surrendered my whole heart, God showed up and saved me from my circumstances!

Amazingly, on July 23, 2013 we were able to move into a brand new house built from the ground up. I was also able to keep the home that Maceo and I had together. It went on the market and a renter fell in love with it and within 30 days there was a rental agreement in place.

Another blessing arrived a year later when I was promoted at work. That promotion came with a higher salary.

With increased finances, I was able to purchase two new vehicles for my family.

Praise God and thank you, Jesus!

My blessings were suddenly overflowing.

And God will generously provide all you need.
Then you will always have everything you need and
plenty left over to share with others.
2 Corinthians 9:8

As you read this book, I want you to realize that God is able to bless you abundantly. In all things, at all times, you can have all that you need; you will abound in every good work.

Over time, I have come to the conclusion that my relationship with the Lord will never waver. I have learned to trust Him more than I ever had before. Reading the Word and spending quality time with God is a way of life for me now. If you haven't developed a closer relationship with Christ, I encourage you to do so right now - today!

Thank you for you having an interest in discovering what the Potluck Blueprint is all about. May your potluck creation be one that will allow you to be filled with goodness of God forever.

Introduction

When I attended Sunday school as a young girl, I learned about Israel and how they misplaced their values. It was God who let them know they would not prosper if they didn't change their ways.

"You have sown much, and harvested little. You eat, but you never have enough; you drink, but you never have your fill. You clothe yourselves, but no one is warm. And he who earns wages does so to put them into a bag with holes. "Thus says the Lord of hosts: Consider your ways. Go up to the hills and bring wood and build the house, that I may take pleasure in it and that I may be glorified, says the Lord. You looked for much, and behold, it came to little. And when you brought it home, I blew it away. Why: declares the Lord of hosts."
Haggai 1:6-9

I like this passage because it demonstrates how important our values are in our lives. Therefore, our first hunger should not be for material possessions, but for spiritual riches through a fellowship with Christ. Because I love God, I am so grateful for His grace and mercy. This love allows me to get my priorities in order so my life will be full and I will have need of nothing.

It is because of my faith that I have been led to this moment to write this book. I have been called to share my lessons, the experiences of my Christian sisters, and the recipes that bring us all together in fellowship for nourishment and growth. *The Potluck Blueprint* is rooted in love, trust, faith, truth and respect for all women across the globe. I know that we are here to help enrich each other's lives through the love of Christ.

As you read through this book, please know that my goal is to fuel all women in the world as they reflect on Christian teachings and fill their bodies with food made with love. I pray that you use this book to enrich your relationship with God and to enhance your encounters with everyone who crosses your path.

We are all called to bring something to the table; and in true potluck fashion, we are not told exactly what must be made. Instead, we are encouraged to bring a dish that reflects our individual skill-set. Everyone benefits when we come in communion with a gift that only we can serve. Just like in life: we are all called to show up with our talents that reflect the blessings from God.

Many of my favorite Scripture passages are at your disposal for spiritual growth and biblical awareness. This book is designed for readers, in every continent, to develop an intimate and rewarding relationship with our Heavenly

Father – God! *The Potluck Blueprint* will provide meaningful Scripture passages to help you develop a well-seasoned foundation for your personal spiritual knowledge and wisdom.   In each chapter there will be inspiring stories from my life, along with authentic stories from other women, a prayer-filled action step from me, and finally a smorgasbord of recipes for yourself and others to feast on.

In addition, in the back of book, there will be space for you to create your own gathering as you fellowship with others to share God's breakthroughs, healings, and victories in your life. There is also an extensive list of music to add to your playlist while you are cooking. The purpose of this book is for you to gain and achieve refreshing fulfillment coupled with a spiritual reward. May God bless you and continue to keep you near Him.

I pray that you recognize your spiritual contributions to the potluck gathering of life. Sharing your gifts in service for others is the ultimate reflection of God's love. May you grow from this book and share it with others so that they, too, may grow in faith and community.

> *In God is my salvation and my glory: the rock of*
> *my strength, and my refuge, is in God.*
> *Psalm 62:7*

Disclaimer: The Bible verses included in this book come from various sources including NIV, AMP, NKJV.

CHAPTER 1

Alignment

You have armed me with strength for battle;
you have humbled my adversaries before me.
Psalms 18:39

We are called into one another's lives to grow and learn, but not always through kindness and support. Some of the most important lessons that I have learned, and which have helped me grow, have come out of unpleasant situations. Through moments of difficulty and inconvenience, we can all learn how strong we truly are.

One of the most distinct "unpleasant" lessons came early in my military career when I was a First Lieutenant. I was assigned to the same barracks with a superior, female Captain for an overnight assignment. This is a common practice within military ranks due to the limited number of women who need housing in a particular situation. I wasn't familiar with this officer, but I knew her to be a respected leader.

On one evening, she answered the door for a male First Lieutenant she supervised who wanted to discuss his evaluation. I was surprised that she let him into our barracks, but didn't question her judgment beyond that because she was in a senior position. After discussing his grievances at length, the young man left with an understanding of how he could improve his standing with the Captain.

The next day, she and I were called into our superior's office. Admittedly I was confused; it was not regular practice for us to be ordered into a meeting as a pair. My confusion quickly switched to anger when I learned that it had been reported that we had hosted a male colleague in our room and had engaged in sexual misconduct with him. I was immediately triggered by these accusations because I knew that I hadn't even been in the same part of the barracks with the man in question. The Colonel was relentless in his conviction that we had displayed poor judgment and had violated policy.

What happened next taught me a lot about myself; in the midst of my formal reprimand, I fought back. I defended my reputation and myself by stating the facts and questioning my anonymous accusers. I eventually turned to the Captain I was bunking with to corroborate the truth of the events, but she stood in silence. She later told me that she didn't feel that the leadership would believe her anyway. She maintained this stance throughout the entire investigation.

I decided early on in this conflict that my reputation was too valuable and my career too new to allow rumors to ruin my potential. Even after that initial conversation in our Colonel's office, I demanded that the truth be revealed. Instead of shrinking from shame and embarrassment, I stood in the conviction that my integrity would be acknowledged.

Eventually the investigation revealed that no wrongdoing had taken place and the accusations had no merit. The Colonel even apologized to me for reprimanding me before getting all of the information about the situation. His level of humility surprised me and I realized how we had both been "sharpened" through this experience. In that moment, I also reflected on how my response differed from the female Captain's. She was more than willing to allow the circumstance, while false, define her image and reputation. She didn't feel she had the ability to stand up for herself even with her rank. I, on the other hand, even as a First Lieutenant, knew I had to defend myself if I was going to be respected and advance in my career. I was "sharpened" through this experience and I learned how to stand in my strength as a woman within a military organization.

I have learned to trust my intuition and show up bravely in situations of adversity. When I stay true to myself and walk with the strength of Christ, I can accomplish all things.

"You're blessed when you stay on course,
walking steadily on the road revealed by God."
Psalm 119:1

Not every trial is accompanied by a workplace sex scandal. Many of my trials as a mother involve my three, high-energy eight year olds and simple things, like breakfast.

Let me explain: I believe in the nourishing power of a warm, healthy breakfast each day. This is a natural desire for any parent, and I am so grateful that I can provide for them in this way. My daughters love when I make them "nutty pancakes," which are pancakes infused with caramel flavor and crushed nuts. They tell me that it's their favorite breakfast offering. This filled me with delight until they asked if they, too, could make the signature recipe.

I'm ashamed to say my immediate desire was to say no to my girls; the time it would take to teach them the proper steps, monitor their every move, and clean-up their mess afterwards made me feel fatigued before any work had actually begun. I know that these are skills I want them to have, but, honestly, I find it difficult to find balance between the desires of three independent girls and my need for efficiency. We all want to be good parents, but priorities need to be established or we would never get anything done.

So does that mean that I never teach my girls my special recipe? I never allow them to experiment and grow if it means I'm inconvenienced? Of course not. But this area of parenting is a challenge for me; I don't always want to step out of my comfort zone and try risky behavior. It takes the grace of God to get me in that kitchen with those beautiful children bouncing and bustling about. It takes a prayerful heart to keep calm in the midst of spills and silliness, but I do it. I become the mother my children need me to be and I guide them through the process of cooking a delicious meal. These moments are adding to their ability to be independent women who can take care of themselves and work well with others. It's an honor to be the one they turn to for guidance.

That being said, I understand that my daughter Traci will try to take over the kitchen and tell everyone, including me, what to do. I also realize that this will probably cause Maci to yell, "You aren't the boss of me." Meanwhile, Staci will avoid the conflict by focusing on the task of stirring and she will probably stir so furiously that batter will spill out and cause a mess that all of us will need to address. I understand these things may happen, but that doesn't change my course. I walk steadily on this path of parenthood as a widowed woman who wants her children to flourish. I know that God shows favor to me in my times of struggle and I know that He will guide me as I attempt to guide my girls. Pancakes will be made!

> *The LORD says, "I will guide you along the best*
> *pathway for your life. I will advise you and*
> *watch over you.*
> *Psalm 32:8*

God has also shown me favor in the writing of this book. For example, when I reached out to several women to contribute their insights and "wisdom," I was surprised how some hesitated and even worried they had no lessons to share. One of my close female friends confessed that she didn't feel that she had a testimony. Here is what she wrote to me:

As I sit here trying to think of a testimony, I wonder what has been my understanding of faith and blessings. It should not be this difficult to give my testimony of the goodness of God in my life. I worry that I have no testimony to offer. You see, I am not a teenage mother, I was never in an abusive relationship that took everything I had to get out, I don't have any addictions to overcome other than binge watching "Law In Order: Special Victims Unit." I have not had any minor or major ailments. My immediate and extended family members are still living, including my 88-year old grandfather. No struggle; no testimony.

That being said, several months ago, I sat in my room, complaining and crying to my heavenly Father about the discontentment I was feeling in my life. I am a single mother, never been married, and a soldier of 23 years, serving in the U.S. Army and Army National Guard. I sometimes feel like I'm in the middle of the ocean treading water. Why am I the tail instead of the head? Why am I beneath instead above? Why am I not the lender instead the borrower? Where is my abundance and overflow? Why am I in a spiritual rut? Why am I still single? Why doesn't my son have an earthly father?

In the midst of my tears and aggravation, the Lord said, "you don't know who you are. What struggles have you had? You excel in all you do. You are "untouchable". The enemy cannot touch you.

You claim you don't have power; the reason why you don't have power is because you gave it to a man. Not because he took it away; you gave it away. So, your frustration is because you are out of touch with Me.

Return to Me."

I am amazed at how powerful her message is, in spite of her claim that she has "no testimony." Whether we are fighting for our reputation on the job, working hard to supervise three small girls in the kitchen, or looking for God in the midst of stagnation, we all have a story to tell.

When we are in alignment, we are able to appreciate our progress and see the future that our Lord has waiting for us. I believe that everyone has a testimony and from our experiences we gain wisdom. Therefore, it is necessary to align with Him so that our message can be shared while growing in His love.

My Prayer:

I thank God, the Father of our Lord Jesus Christ that we are humble to ourselves and others. That we remember to delight in weak moments and difficult times. For when we are weak, then we will be made strong.

I pray that you will take time today to reflect on your alignment and how you choose to respond to those who challenge your sense of peace. How do you stay on the path when there are so many distractions and frustrations along the way?

"Fear not, for I am with you; be not dismayed, for I am your God; I will strengthen you, I will help you, I will up hold you with my righteous right hand."

Isaiah 41:10

* The following is the first of seven authentic and vulnerable stories entitled "Wisdom from Women" at the end of each chapter. These stories are from real women who have grown in their faith through their trials and personal hardships. I hope that you are blessed by each one!

-Wisdom from Women-

"He heals the brokenhearted and binds
up their wounds."
Psalm 147:3

"Abigail" - Age 22

I remember sitting on a bench in a courthouse lob-
by when I was a teen. A female social worker silently ap-
proached me and sat beside me. The woman kindly told me
who she was and explained that my cousin, who was my
guardian at the time, had decided to give up her rights to
the state and that I would be going into the foster care sys-
tem. She then asked me if I was okay with that decision. Out
of hurt and anger, I vaguely processed the idea of no longer
being in the care of the woman I was living with, and nod-
ded my head in approval. There were so many thoughts and
emotions whirling within me, that, at the time, I wasn't re-
ally focusing on what exactly was transpiring around me.
My primary thought was, "where am I going to live next?"

Ever since I was born, and with every few passing years
prior to foster care, I lived with multiple family relatives for
different reasons. Sometimes it was because of my volatile
home environment and other times it was because my

family members and I had relocated; abrupt moves were a way of life. On some level, I had become accustomed to moving from one relative's house to another.

My parents weren't in a stable position to provide for me, so my maternal grandparents raised me for the majority of my childhood life. When my grandparents decided to move to another state, I went to live with my cousins for a couple years. I happily lived with my grandparents again during my middle school years. Things shifted for me when it was close to the time for me to go into high school. I started feeling the loneliness of not being with my mom. At that point, I moved back to Michigan to be near to my mother and to build a better relationship with her. She was still unstable at this point, so I was living with a cousin. It wasn't ideal, but I was grateful that I could see her on a regular basis.

For a while, things were great. I excelled in my first year of high school: I was socially secure, quite healthy, emotionally happy, and thankful for all of my blessings. Around the beginning of my second year of high school, my mother was hospitalized for chronic back pain. Doctors soon discovered something more severe with her health and she had to undergo open-heart surgery. We briefly hoped for a full recovery. Unfortunately, during a second procedure the doctors realized there was nothing they could do to save her. She had an infection in her blood stream that was killing *her slowly, and her organs were failing. My mother suffered through extreme pain and discomfort. There was no way to stop her heart from pumping the toxic blood through her veins unless she was going to live on a machine for the rest of her life. On the 22nd of October in the year of 2007, my mother, my angel, went to heaven to live eternally in spirit. I was 14 years old at the time and it was very detrimental. I can see now that it has impacted all aspects of my life.*

I can admit that the initial mourning over the loss of mother became destructive. This may have been the reason my cousin gave up her guardianship rights to the state. I also wonder if there were other options besides foster care, but at the time, I assume everyone thought it was the best move. Of course, I contacted other relatives, but my reputation proceeded me and I wasn't offered an alternate housing option within the family.

Being in foster care was no 'walk-in-the-park;' it was more like a walk through the woods in the dark. There were some positive experiences sprinkled throughout that time. I was able to attend a girls' camp that taught character building, healthy relationship development, and trust and teamwork skills. I participated in talent shows and pageants and received care that was funded from different sponsors associated with the foster care agency. There were many different situations that supported my growth in personal independence and appreciating sisterhood. I never would've had these opportunities if I were still living with my actual relatives.

Even though I was living in foster care, I was not the typical foster youth stereotype. This is because I spent the majority of my life in better homes and good schools and positive influences; so the environment that I came from was a lot different from most foster youth who experienced something more negative. I was blessed to be introduced to people who wanted the best for me; they consistently helped guide me with skills that were necessary for me to succeed in the future.

The relationship between my father and I improved during this time because it felt necessary after the loss of my mother. (My father had always been around for the majority of my life, but usually from a distance). As I advanced through the foster care programs, the connection with my father was a saving grace in my life.

There were times during my teen years when I ran away from home with no knowledge of where I would end up. I had faith that I would figure it out, or God would somehow get me through it.

The LORD is my light and my salvation--so why should I be afraid? The LORD is my fortress, protecting me from danger, so why should I tremble?
Psalm 27:1

The faith of my childhood became even stronger when I got into foster care. Since I had been living in Christian households up to that point, it never escaped my heart that God had a purpose for me. I had always been involved with my religion; being active in churches, doing community services, praying by myself, with my family, and even at school. There was always something and someone around me that constantly reminded me of all of God's ability and His promise.

The LORD is my shepherd,
I shall not want.
He makes me lie down in green pastures;
He leads me beside quiet waters.
He restores my soul;
He guides me in the paths of righteousness
For His name's sake.
Psalm 23:1-3

My grandmother enforced the Bible, my cousins encouraged church and community activity, my family supported prayer, and my counselors insured all of the above. In the end, it all helped me to align with God's Grace. Throughout my life, I have been a witness to God's graciousness and the power of prayer. With every challenge that I have encountered so far, it has forced me and my faith to become stronger. I know that not only do I have the strength to become better, but I serve a purpose here on Earth as my gift back to God.

I encourage everyone who has dealt with hardship and challenges to really know that with God and within you, everything will be fine. No matter how hard it may seem; as long as we follow through with what God requires of us, and always believe, God will bring you through it.

He will cover you with his feathers.
He will shelter you with his wings.
His faithful promises are your
armor and protection.
Psalm 91:4

I have learned that I must remain in gratitude and continue to live life God's way in order to receive the promise of prosperity in all ways.

Do not ever stop believing. With time and experience, you will notice more of His love for you and it is up to you to show your love back to Him by not allowing anything to give you doubt of His power. Stay in His word and stay true because it is guaranteed to work out in your favor.

Therefore, humble yourselves under the mighty
hand of God, that He may exalt you at the
proper time, casting all your anxiety on Him,
because He cares for you.
1 Peter 5:6-7

-Relationship Recipes-

Join the family together at breakfast

Nutty Yummy Pancakes

1 ½ c flour

3 tbsp sugar

1 ½ tsp baking powder

½ tsp salt

¼ tsp nutmeg

1 tsp baking soda

1c and 2 tbsp Carnations milk

½ tsp vanilla extract

½ tsp caramel extract or flavor

4 tbsp melted butter

1 egg

1 c chopped pecans or walnuts (to taste)

Whisk dry ingredients in a bowl. Add in milk, vanilla and caramel, whisk until blended. In a separate bowl, mix butter and egg; fold into the flour mixture until just combined. Add chop pecans or walnuts in batter or on top. Pour mixture in preheated, greased skillet until bubbles appear. Cook until golden brown.

Serve with butter and maple syrup.

Scrambled Omelet

1 tsp cayenne pepper

1 tsp onion powder

1 tsp lemon pepper

Diced green and/or red bell pepper

Diced onion

1 chopped mushroom

2-3 slices of cheese

Pet milk (enough to cover bottom of bowl)

2 eggs

Mix all ingredients into a bowl. Spray skillet with pam. Add 1 tbsp of butter and let melt in pan. Pour omelet into pan, let sit and cook for 2-3 min and scramble together.

Glazed Sausage Bites

1 slightly beaten eggs

1 lb pork sausage

½ c finely crushed saltine crackers (14)

¼ c milk

½ tsp rubbed sage

½ c water

¼ c ketchup

2 tbsp brown sugar

1 tbsp vinegar

1 tbsp soy sauce

In mixing bowl, combine egg, sausage, crackers, milk, and sage. Beat at high speed on electric mixture for 5 min. Shape into 1 ¼ inch balls. Mixture will be soft. Wet hands to shape easily. In skillet, brown meat in all sides, shaking pan occasionally to keep balls round, about 10 min. Pour off excess fat. Combine water, ketchup, brown sugar, vinegar and soy sauce. Pour over meatballs. Cover and simmer 15 min, stirring occasionally. Keep hot until ready to serve. Makes 3 dozen balls.

Louisiana Salmon Croquette

1 can of red salmon
1 yellow onion, chopped fine
1 bell pepper chopped fine
2 slices of bread
1 medium white potato, boiled and mashed
1 egg
1 tsp black pepper
yellow corn meal

Combine first 7 ingredients until well-blended. Shape into patties. Coat in cornmeal and fry in hot oil, turning once. Lay on paper towels to drain. Serve hot. Makes 4 patties.

CHAPTER 2

Balance

"And be not conformed to this world: but be transformed
by the renewing of your mind, that you may prove what [is]
that good, and acceptable, and perfect, will of God."
Romans 12:2

When I lost my husband, Maceo, and he went to be with the Lord, I developed a stronger relationship with his aunt who lives in North Carolina. She and I talked for hours during that difficult time. We discussed family challenges, career plans, friendship goals, and our spiritual growth. She has taught me so much about how to find balance in my life despite the turbulent experiences I'd gone through. I remember her telling me:

"Our daily lives revolve around our family life, our social life with friends, our work life and hopefully our spiritual or church life. These aspects of our daily lives create interactions, pressures and constant decisions as to how to navigate through all of the situations presented by these combined aspects of our lives. These relationships can cause issues to say the least. We do not get to choose our family; we are given family and have to learn how to balance conflicting ideas in order to maintain a peaceful existence. On the other hand, we get to choose our friends. We get to choose our work environment. We control our spiritual life or church life.

Life has been good because I keep striving to make the right choices in the areas where I *can* decide. Daily prayer is a skill that I developed early in my life for guidance in making decisions and analyzing the various scenarios that will result from my actions. I pray for both faith and courage to stay focused and to follow through with the best choice in any situation. Life has shown me that even if the decision seems less than ideal, through continued prayer and faith, God will lead me to the ultimate good and the blessings will show up for my highest good."

We all have the ability to choose God in every aspect of life. His love, and His love alone, will help us to stay in balance despite the challenges that surround us.

Sadly, even though we have access to God's guidance, I see imbalance all around me. There are hearts that are hurting because they cannot find any place of peace that exists within the extremes of human existence. In order to find balance in this earthly classroom, we must have the unique gifts that God has provided for us within our reach.

I had to be reminded of this lesson while at work last week. I was focused on an assignment until my entire consciousness became consumed with hunger. Out of no-where, I couldn't think about anything but food. I looked in my workbag for some snacks, but surprisingly, I didn't have anything with me that day.

"No snacks! What was I thinking?" I muttered to my-self.

My irritation was steadily increasing as my stomach started to clench. At this point I decided to focus all of my energy on the hunt for sustenance and I stood up from my desk. Abandoning my work for a snack made perfect sense to me at the time; I was hungry! As I wandered out of my office and down the hallway, I looked at my coworkers not as fellow humans, but as potential snack providers.

"Hey Doug, do you happen to have a snack I could share?"

"No, sorry."

I gave Doug a forced smile and a nod in appreciation as I continued on my mission. Barbara wasn't in her of-fice; Barbara always had snacks. Sigh. I continued down the hallway towards our break room. The large vending machine was still offline and in need of repairs. Ah, but the small vending machine was working!

I put my money in the smaller machine and made my selection with a relieved sigh. My anguish was starting to subside and I began imagining the food tantalizing my mouth and then satisfying my belly.

The circular arm of the vending machine slowly wound around and around and I saw my treat get closer to the edge of the interior shelf. I held my breath when I realized it wasn't moving forward far enough to actually fall. Then the motor stopped, and my snack stayed stubbornly in its position instead of falling down to where I could retrieve it.

My exhale was long and angry. The machine had eaten my money which meant I wouldn't be eating anything. It wasn't fair. I almost cried. A grown woman, in a comfortable work environment, who had eaten breakfast only a few hours prior, almost started crying because she couldn't get a snack.

I suddenly took stock of my situation and thought about my out-of-control frustration. I realized that I was getting caught up in a scenario that I wanted to control, but couldn't. I was out of balance and felt terrible. I took another breath; a long, prayerful breath. I asked God to give me comfort and I remembered what I had learned from the Bible:

"Do not be anxious about your life, what you will eat, nor about your body, what you will put on. For life is more than food, and the body more than clothing. Consider the ravens: they neither sow nor reap, they have neither storehouse nor barn and yet God feeds them. Of how much more value are

you than the birds! And which of you by being anxious can add a single hour to his span of life? If then you are not able to do as small a thing as that why are you anxious about the rest? Consider the lilies, how they grow: they neither toil nor spin, yet I tell you, even Solomon in all his glory was not arrayed like one of these. But if God so clothes the grass, which is alive in the field today, and tomorrow is thrown into the oven, how much more will he clothe you, O you of little faith! And do not seek what you are to eat and what you are to drink, nor be worried. For all the nations of the world seek after these things and your Father knows that you need them. Instead, seek his kingdom, and these things will be added to you."
Luke 12:22-31.

After reciting these words in my head and understanding them in my heart, I felt a sense of peace in my stomach. I was no longer desperate for physical food and I could feel a sense of calm fill me.

As I turned to walk back to my office and the work that I had left behind, I saw my boss standing in the doorway.

"Hey, Rhonda! I made some of my famous coffee cake and brought in grapes and beverages. Would you like to make yourself a plate and have a quick snack?"

I smiled graciously and accepted the unexpected invitation. How anxious I was only a few minutes ago! Now

I had a new level of trust in God. Not only does He provide in all things, but he allows us to experience important lessons in our daily lives. We are given tests that help our growth as we seek answers for the big and small questions of life.

I know that I don't have to seek the answers right away, but I do know that I need to call on God when I feel lost. Because God has given us many "tools" to navigate life, we are expected to use them when we feel tested by our circumstances.

When I first read, "Heaven's Grocery Story," I realized that the "tools" we need as we spread the word of God's love are simple: patience, love, and understanding. Of course, this poem explores other virtues as well, but starting with those three can make all the difference.

Heaven's Grocery Store

Marching down life's highway, my feet became very sore

I then came upon a sign that read "Heaven's Grocery Store".

When I got closer the doors swung open wide.

Next thing I knew I was standing there inside

I saw a flock of angels positioned everywhere.

They handed me a basket and said, "Child, shop with care."

Everything a human required was in that grocery store.

With many commodities to carry, you could always come back for more.

THE POTLUCK BLUEPRINT

First I acquired some Patience; Love was in that same row.

Further down was Understanding, you require that everywhere you go.

I grabbed a box of Wisdom and Faith, a bag or two

And obtained Charity of course but more than just a few

And then reached for Courage to help me run this wicked race.

My basket was almost full but I remembered some loving Grace

I then chose Salvation for it was advertised as free

I tried to collect enough of that for both you and me.

Then I started to the counter to pay my grocery bill,

For I thought I had everything to do the Master's will.

As I went up the aisle, I saw Prayer and proceeded to put that in.

For I knew when I stepped outside I was bound to encounter sin.

Peace and Joy were plentiful, the last thing on that shelf

Song and Praise were hanging near so I just helped myself.

Then I asked an angel, "Now how much do I owe?"

She smiled and said, "Just take them wherever you may go."

Again I asked, "No really, how much do I owe?"

"My child," she said, "God paid your bill a long time ago."

– Author Unknown

Too often we think we don't have what it takes to help others, but when we truly reflect on what we need to support our community members and navigate the road ahead, we realize how simple it really can be.

I find balance between my roles as a woman, mother, military employee, church member, friend, and family member by grounding myself in the consistent truth of God's word. I know that if I am a virtuous woman in all things, my soul, my career, and all of my other roles will be blessed. To say that in another way; if I can be 100% a child of God regardless of my position or location, I can find a balance between what my role demands and what my soul needs. It doesn't matter if my job is stressful, my children are demanding, or my family is feuding. If I can keep my mind and heart focused on gratitude, for the gifts I have already received, I can navigate the treacherous path before me.

Last night I wrote this letter of gratitude to God, I suggest you write one yourself so that you can recognize all the tools and blessings you *already* have in your life.

Dear God:

Thank You for granting me...

knowledge and wisdom

anointed favor over my life, children, family and friends

strength and courage through all life's trials and tribulations

victory in all battles

super-natural healing; emotional, physical, mental, spiritual, and financial

peace that can surpass my understanding

shelter from the rain and storms of life

promises for all things to work for my good when I'm standing upright

compassion for others

a heart to serve

the mighty force to overpower all the evil that tries to come against
me and the people I love

the tranquility inside of me and the beacon of light to help guide
others in darkness

Your will to be done

grace and mercy coupled with your love to overcome the impossible

Amen.

While gratitude and gifts are important, ultimately, I believe that there are twelve areas in our life that require our attention They are our health and fitness, our intellectual life, our emotional life, our character, our spiritual life, our romantic relationships, our parenting vision, our social life, our financial life, our quality of life, and our life vision. If you would like to further explore your life and balance through these specific areas, answer the following in your mind or in a journal.

Your Spiritual Life

How often do you meditate or pray?

How often do you go to church?

Intellectual Life

How many books do you want to read every month or yearly?

How many languages do you want to learn to speak?
What new skills do you want to have?
How do you want to grow yourself professionally?

Emotional life
How do you deal with stress and anger?
How do you maintain happiness in the now?

Health and fitness
How do you want your body and health to look like?

Your Character
What are your values?
What do you believe in?
What type of person do you want to be?
Do you want to be the kind of person who stands by their word?

Love Relationship
Who do you want to wake up with every morning?
What does that relationship look like?
What do you do together?
How do you spend time together?

Parenting Vision

How many kids do you want to create?

What kind of parents do you want to be?

What values do you want to teach your children?

How do you spend time with your kids?

Your Social Life

Who are your friends?

Who do you hang out with?

When do you hang out with them?

How do you support each other?

Your Financial Life

How much cash do you have in the bank?

What could you afford?

What are your financial goals for the next 5-10 years: savings, retirement plans, business investments?

Your Career

What do you want to create, build, or grow?

What is the next promotion you are aiming for?

What's the next company you want to build?

What's the next blog or book you want to produce?

Your Quality of Life

What types of hotels do you want to stay in?

How often can you travel business class?

What would your ideal home look like?

What does your office look like?

How do you dress?

How often can you take vacations?

Your Life Visions

What is your vision for your future?

My Prayer:

I thank God, the Father of our Lord Jesus Christ that we may live a life worthy of the Lord and we please Him in every way: bearing-fruit in every good work, growing in the knowledge of God.

I pray that you look at specific areas of your life through the eyes of God and ask for guidance as you strive for balance in all aspects of your daily routine. How are you using the tools and blessings that you already have to live your life's divine purpose?

Take 10 minutes to meditate and then write a letter of gratitude to God.

Wise choices will watch over you.
Understanding will keep you safe.
Proverbs 2:11

-Wisdom from Women-

"I will also speak of your testimonies before kings
and shall not be put to shame."
Psalm 119:46

"Bernice"- age 40

Some would say that I am a product of a mess. My mom was married to a man other than my father and my father was married to another woman. It was a chance meeting between the two of them that became a deep, passionate, forbidden kind of love. When I showed up in the mid 70's, the secret was revealed, and so went two marriages down the drain. There was a lot of bitterness and anger and with other children in the picture for both my mother and father, a lot of heartache. Yet, the reality was that they had me so they decided to give their relationship a try. I wish I could say that from there it was a happily ever after kind of ending, but it was far from it. Before I turned one my mother was homeless, alone, and trying desperately to cope with the fact that my father had returned to his wife. Yet, my mother held on to my father and for 10 years endured a very volatile, unstable, emotionally and physically abusive relationship.

As a young girl, my definition of marriage was based on lies, deceit, jealousy, and, sadly, abuse. My ideas were influenced partially by the relationship my mother endured with my father, but more so because she continued to date married men. From childhood through adulthood, my father's presence was unstable and emotionally distant. Because of this, my idea of a father was shaped by inconsistency and disappointment.

What my father lacked in love, my mother more than made up for; she loved me unconditionally. She doted on me and made me feel special. To her, I was a true scholar, beyond creative, and extremely talented. In her eyes, I was brilliant which was a tremendous boost for my self-esteem. Although I was a product of her mistakes she reminded me that I was not a mistake. I came from love. As a single parent, she offered as much support, protection, and stability that she could. She instilled in me the power of knowing who I am and my self-worth. By the 80's, she was heavily involved in the church and a Sunday School teacher. From that point on, our lives were shaped by her love for God. She instilled in me the importance of affirmations and prayer. I was constantly reminded that God is our only true Provider and my only true Father. In the mist of what felt chaotic at times: the lack of a father figure, the lack of money, growing up in the inner city, I also had a sense of peace. My mother would say we have to thank God for what's Right, not for what's Wrong. So, through my mother's walk with God, I became validated in Spirit, which is a precious gift to give a child.

The lessons my mother taught me resonate with me today. I am reminded that God doesn't just give you what you ask for, but what you envision is yours by divine right. If you think small, you will receive little, but if you think big, you will be magnificently blessed. So, when it came to my own life, I realized that I had to envision the type of life I wanted to live which directly supports my self-worth.

For example, when I was in college, I prayed for the type of man I wanted in my life and I knew what type of father he would be. Twenty-one years later, I am with the same man and our marriage is one of friendship, laughter, love, and commitment. Our success is due, in part, to the vision we had of what our marriage would be together. What helps us is that we continue to work and affirm that vision.

The choices I made and the relationships I have had along the way led me here, and I am so thankful. I know that GOD is all that there is and He lives within me. He is my true Father, my true Protector, and my true Provider. My life has been abundant not only because of my wishes, hopes and dreams, but because I knew God had the power to make them come true.

I don't just speak these words, but I know them to be true. For the last 10 years I have owned my own business *and have assisted parents and students with accomplishing their educational goals. I know that being an educator is something that God created me to be. The passion that I have towards my students' success and academic milestones has been rewarding.*

Throughout my adult life, I have met so many extraordinary people in my quest to leave my imprint on the world. I have also had doors and opportunities open to me because I am doing God's work. Furthermore, I have had the pleasure to travel and obtain a deeper perspective of God's wonders. Thankfully, my husband has been a tremendous supporter and our relationship has flourished. Our children have a great sense of love, family, and faith. Through life's joys and tribulations, I remain happy and unyielding in my love for God and my walk with Him.

-Relationship Recipes-

Bring the family together for salads

Greek Pasta Salad

1 box of dry pasta (any shape)
2c chopped broccoli
1c Kalamata olives, sliced
1c crumbled feta cheese
1 cucumber, diced
2c tomatoes, diced
1c Greek salad dressing (or to taste)
Grilled salmon or chicken (optional)
Cook pasta according to instructions on the box. Mix drained pasta and toss with remaining ingredients. Serve at room temperature or chilled

Broccoli & Relish Salad

4 c chopped broccoli
8 slices bacon crisp
¼ c raisins
¼ c radish
1 small onion, chopped small
1 c mayonnaise
3 tbsp vinegar
¼ c sugar

Mix together broccoli, bacon, raisins, radish, and add mayonnaise. In bowl, mix vinegar and sugar, add onions, then, pour over broccoli mixture. Place in refrigerator for 24 hours.

Cold Vegetable Salad

1 large can French-style string beans

1 large can LeSueur Peas

1 can shoepeg corn

1 jar pimentos

1 c chopped celery

1 large green pepper, chopped

½ c sugar

½ c vinegar

½ c oil

1 tsp salt

1 tsp pepper

Drain canned vegetables, combine all ingredients in a bowl. Chill and serve. Serves 8.

CHAPTER 3

Core

"Though you have not seen him, you love him;
and even though you do not see him now,
you believe in him and are filled with an
inexpressible and glorious joy."
1 Peter 1:8

We cannot physically see our heavenly Father, but his love is ever-present and can support us at all times. If we allow Him to be at the center, or core, of our existence, we will be blessed with peace and guidance. That being said, we are also called to find companions to travel with us during our earthly journey. When we seek a spouse, we must start with God.

As a woman, and now as a widow, I understand the power of companionship. The relationship between partners, spouses, co-parents, or simply lovers, can deeply impact all aspects of one's life. Both before and after my two marriages, I have had a variety of relationships. Some lifted my heart to God and some hid me away from His light. I have experienced heartbreak and loneliness. Men have promised me love and, instead, lured me into controlling relationships that fed their ego and not my soul. Time and again, I have opened my life to men who have not proven themselves worthy to me or my faith.

From these experiences I have learned that at the core there is only God. He must be first. He needs to be at the center, beginning, and foundation of all relationships. I now know this to be true, but in the past, I didn't apply this complete truth to my life. I used to allow myself to fall in love with a man and have my heart broken by a love that was imperfect and human. I realize now, that when I forgot my core relationship with God, no other relationship had a chance.

So as I move forward in prayerful search for a man who can be a worthy spouse to me and powerful guide for my three daughters, I pray in thoughts and through writing. If you don't already journal, I suggest that you try it; especially when you are distraught about a situation that you feel is bigger than yourself. That moment of despair is the perfect time to call on the Father and lay your concerns at His feet. You do not need to wait until the hurt consumes you, in addition, you can also call on Him when you are at a crossroads and simply desire peace as you move forward on your path.

Here is an example of a letter I wrote in my journal:
Dear Father in Heaven,

I think a met a wonderful man. Father, please reveal to me if he is my future husband. If you say Yes, I thank you for this man. If you say No, I still thank you for allowing me to have an opportunity to meet someone new- but I will need for you to set my mind and thoughts elsewhere and move forward without delay, regret, or resentment.

God, while hoping that he is my husband, I ask you to protect his mind, heart, and his comings and goings. Most importantly, guard his love and compassion to serve you and help others. Right now he has shown me that he is of good character and I truly admire that quality in him.

Father, if he is intended as my future husband, touch his spirit and let him not waiver in his potential position. Speak to him so clearly and boldly as you spoke to Joseph (when Mary was carrying Jesus.) We both desire to have a marriage that glorifies You. I just would like to know with complete clarity if he is the chosen one for me and the future daddy for my girls.

I know that a man must hear directly from you, but I'm not sure if he has even asked you about me. Therefore, I know it is important to write it down as you required in Habakkuk 2:2-3: "Record the vision and inscribe it on tablets, that the one who reads it may run. For the vision is yet for the appointed time; It hastens toward the goal and it will not fail. Though it tarries, wait for it; for it will certainly come, it will not delay."

Please allow me to enjoy the journey filling my days with laughter until You answer my request. I know that everything happens with Divine timing and I will stay faithful and patient as everything unfolds as you wish.

Thank you God and in Jesus' name I say- Amen!

I wrote that entry because I no longer wanted to worry if this man was the right one for me and my family. Do you ever have a worry that feels too big for your heart? A decision too important to make on your own? It is during these times that we must lay down our egos and our sense of power and allow a greater, all-knowing guide into our consciousness.

When you take time to pray, you allow another level of wisdom to enter your heart. I have experienced this level of peace when I stop my worrying and focus on peace through my spiritual connection. Sometimes that means I am alone and on my knees beside my bed, praying as I have since I was a child. Other times I hold the hands of my girls and ask for grace to enter our family and continue to bless and guide us. Occasionally I will receive the wisdom of God as I lie awake in bed in the middle of the night or as I drive to work through endless traffic. I have learned that you can call on God for support and insight while with your church family or in the middle of a staff meeting at work.

There is no time when you cannot connect to the core of your existence and the primary relationship in your life. You have no limits or restrictions within the spiritual relationship you have with your Creator. Whether in word, thought, or writing, He is *with* you and *for* you in all things. You are allowed to suffer in your independent thinking or you can turn over your hardships to Him and ask that all problems be resolved through His glory.

Have you ever had a moment in your life when you didn't think you would ever be able to love again? Can you remember crying excessively, mourning daily, or even screaming out in emotional anguish? I have lived through pain myself and I can relate to your suffering. When we are hurting this badly, we must pray. When we commune with God, something happens within our hearts and we realize we have had our perfect companion by our side all along.

Let me explain in a different way, the love that we seek in the world is the promise of God within us. He desires to pour Himself into us as love and understanding. It is we who close the door upon this flood of goodness by our own acceptance of loneliness.

I asked God to please forgive me, and in that moment, I also forgave myself. I had been expecting my life to be perfect and I had been determined to create that perfection myself. It was time I accepted help and released my mind from the decision-making that stemmed from my ego instead of from my faith.

At that same time, I resolved to turn my back on feelings of rejection, isolation, and abandonment. I remembered that I was the beloved child of the Father and nothing could separate me from His Love. I knew, to the core of my being, that as I allowed this perfect, all-embracing love to flourish within, it would become manifest in my life.

And it has!

I know now that God is loving me as my perfect companion. On a daily basis I say, "Thank you so much for caring for me in spite of my choices and my causal behavior towards you."

The God I serve knows how to bring us together in a perfect way. All that I need is contained in His Love. God is my father, mother, brother, husband, and friend. Therefore, I thank you Father, that you have given me Yourself. I trust You to send me the one You have chosen for me in Your time. Until then, may I rest in Your love alone.

> *"I have loved you with an everlasting love;*
> *I have drawn you with unfailing kindness."*
> *Jeremiah 31:3*

The poet James Weldon Johnson saw the "loneliness" of God. God was all might, yet He longed to have fellowship with a creature made in His image. In creating man, God took the greatest gamble in the universe. Man could bring God great happiness or deep sorrow. As we hold a newborn baby in our arms, we realize that a child has the ability to become the greatest joy in our life, or the greatest sorrow we could ever know. This tiny baby has the power to make us extremely proud of him, or desperately embarrassed. So when God created man and breathed life into him, God exposed himself to the possibility of the creation hurting Him deeply. Yet He loved and took the chance. Johnson captures this in his beautiful poem, "The Creation"

> **God said: I'm lonely still.**
> **Then God sat down-**
> **On the side of a hill where He could think:**
> **By a deep, wide river He sat down:**
> **With His head in His hands,**
> **God thought and thought,**
> **Till He thought: I'll make Me a man!**
> **Up from the bed of the river**
> **God scooped the clay:**
> **And by the bank of the river**
> **He kneeled Him down:**
> **And there the Great God Almighty**
> **Who lit the sun and fixed it in the sky,**
> **Who flung the stars to the most far**
> **corner of the night,**
> **Who rounded the earth in the middle of His hand:**

This Great God,
Like a mammy bending over her baby,
Kneeling down in the dust
Toiling over a clump of clay
Till He shaped it in His own image;
Then into it He blew the breath of life,
And man became a living soul.

I love this poem, it conveys God's essence is at our very core. Therefore, it is imperative that we stay connected to Him in all of our decisions because we are His creation. Unfortunately, I didn't seek this connection as a young adult when I chose to marry my first husband. I failed to consult my father before we eloped.

Although the poem references only the creation of the man, the Bible teaches us that God looked at His creation of man and saw it was good. It was later that God took notice that something beautiful was missing. That's when God decided to create woman. When God completed His work; Adam became excited with these words:

"This is now bone of my bones, and flesh of my flesh: she shall be called Woman, because she was taken out of Man."
Genesis 2:23

Right there is when we discover that it takes both male and female to make humanity. God takes it a step further and now creates marriage. This is when the male and female become one flesh. Each gender completes one another and two people can become together what they could never be alone.

I didn't ask God or my earthly father for consent for my first marriage. I did not consider his thoughts or opinions on the matter. As his daughter, I was totally out of order.

"Ask and it will be given to you, seek and you will find, knock and it will be open to you."
Matthew 7:7

My spirit later told me if I had allowed God to choose my husband I would not have had the trail of emotional, physical and mental abuse at the tender age of 20. At that time, I married a man that my family hardly knew. I knew him for four months and married the next month. I wasn't pregnant, but we rushed into marriage because I was smitten and charmed by him. Our first year of marriage was spent apart; he was active military and assigned to Fort Bragg in North Carolina while I finished college in Norfolk, Virginia. When we finally moved in together, we relocated to Fort Benning, Georgia, which was farther away from my friends and family. I soon learned that he had a quick temper and was extremely controlling. Since I didn't know him well before we got married, this behavior was a surprise to me. It was like living with Dr. Jekyll and Mr. Hyde; he would praise me one minute and tear me down the next. I was never one to be controlled, so this dynamic was stifling, to say the least.

My husband became mentally abusive and that soon transitioned to physical abuse. I was embarrassed that this could happen to me and I was hesitant to tell my father that I had picked a partner who would treat me this way. In fact, my family didn't know the truth about my husband's behavior until after I decided to divorce him five years later. I am an independent and private person, so it felt natural to handle the negativity of my marriage by myself.

Even after my experiences with my first husband, I believe God's will is for marriage to provide an atmosphere of warmth and tenderness. He wants marriage, at its core, to be an environment where a couple can learn to give their love without being hurt or taken advantage of. Most importantly the home should help to develop those Christlike characteristics that God wants us to have. I took none of this into account nor did I seek counsel before making this life-changing decision as a young adult.

Ultimately, I ended up being a divorcee by the age of 25, right around the time my childhood friends were starting to get married. Internally, I was feeling like a failure. I never thought I would be another statistic of divorce. To be honest, it bothered me for many years.

By the age of 27 I had an epiphany, God said "Honor your father and your mother, so that you may live long in the land the LORD your God is giving you." (Exodus 20:12) I took hold of that Scripture and walked in boldness. That following Sunday I attended my childhood church with my dad and rededicated my life back to Christ. Although that may have been enough to get on track, I didn't stop there. I remember turning to my pastor and asking him if it was okay for my dad to come forward and join me at the church altar. With thoughts of regret and tears of joy, I asked my daddy for his forgiveness. I needed to make amends for the hurt, disappointment, and shame I caused him by being disobedient.

That was the right thing for me to do, and from that moment on, my dad and I have had a much stronger and loving relationship because of my obedience in yielding to the voice of God.

I encourage everyone to seek God first to hear what He wants from you. This advice has served me well even before my first marriage; when I was a college freshman.

As soon as I entered college, I decided to join the Army ROTC program. Later, on the day of my college graduation, not only did I walk across the stage to get my Bachelor's Degree, I also earned my commission as a 2nd Lieutenant for the United States Army.

Thinking back, it was during my studies in Military Science that I learned the Army's seven core values. The core values are what Army members are expected to know and live by professionally *and* personally. I'm sure the private industry has policies and procedures that are to be followed; however, when you go home, your professional character doesn't have to follow you. Right?

Well, not in the Army. The Army values are: loyalty, duty, respect, selfless service, honor, integrity, and personal courage. Members of the Army are expected to carry out these values daily at work and at home. I'm always impressed how people recognize those who are in uniform. It's amazing that every time I go out in public while wearing my fatigues, strangers thank me for my service. There is so much support for our military values that I think it's worth looking at here.

Soldier members are expected to demonstrate the following, at all times:

1. Loyalty – Bear true faith and allegiance to the U.S. Constitution, the Army, your unit and other soldiers. Bearing true faith and allegiance is a matter of believing in and devoting yourself to something or someone. A loyal soldier is one who supports the leadership and stands up for fellow soldiers. By wearing the uniform of the U.S. Army, you are expressing your loyalty. By doing your share, you show your loyalty to your unit.

2. Duty- Fulfill your obligations. Doing your duty means more than carrying out your assigned tasks. Duty means being able to accomplish tasks as part of a team. The work of the U.S. Army is a complex combination of missions, tasks and responsibilities – all in constant motion. Our work entails building one assignment onto another. You fulfill your obligations as a part of your unit every time you resist the temptation to take "shortcuts" that might undermine the integrity of the final product.

3. Respect – Treat people as they should be treated. In the Soldier's Code, we pledge to "treat others with dignity and respect while expecting others to do the same." Respect is what allows us to appreciate the best in other people. Respect is trusting that all people have done their jobs and fulfilled their duty. The Army is one team and each of us has something to contribute.

4. Selfless Service – Put the welfare of the nation, the Army and your subordinates before your own. Selfless service is larger than just one person. In serving your country, you are doing your duty loyally without thought of recognition or gain. The basic building block of selfless service is the commitment of each team member to go a little further, endure a little longer, and look a little closer to see how he or she can add to the effort.

5. Honor – Live up to Army values. The nation's highest military award is The Medal of Honor. This award goes

to Soldiers who make honor a matter of daily living – Soldiers who develop the habit of being honorable, and solidify that habit with every value choice they make. Honor is a matter of carrying out, acting, and living the values of respect, duty, loyalty, selfless service, integrity and personal courage in everything you do.

6. Integrity – Do what's right, legally and morally. Integrity is a quality you develop by adhering to moral principles. It requires that you do and say nothing that deceives others. As your integrity grows, so does the trust others place in you. The more choices you make based on integrity, the more this highly prized value will affect your relationships with family and friends, and, finally, the fundamental acceptance of yourself.

7. Personal Courage – Face fear, danger or adversity (physical or moral). Personal courage has long been associated with our Army. With physical courage, it is a matter of enduring physical safety. Facing moral fear or adversity may be a long, slow process of continuing forward on the right path, especially if taking those actions is not popular with others. You can build your personal courage daily by standing up for, and acting upon the things that you know are honorable.

I must say in my twenty-four years of wearing the uniform, there have been times when I struggled in executing all of my core values. The one value that I believe I was born with, that also naturally fits my character, is loyalty. I have seen this trait shine through some of the most difficult times in my career and personal life.

In the Bible, King David gives us the guidelines for incorporating loyalty. We can all relate this Scripture to our core values.

In Psalm 15 it says,

"Lord, who may dwell in your sacred tent? Who may live on your holy mountain? The one whose walk is blameless, who does what is righteous, who speaks the truth from their heart; whose tongue utters no slander, who does no wrong to a neighbor, and casts no slur on others; who despises a vile person but honors those who fear the Lord; who keeps an oath even when it hurts, and does not change their mind; who lends money to the poor without interest; who does not accept a bribe against the innocent. Whoever does these things will never be shaken."

Serving in the military and being married have tested my faith in the same way that all of us are challenged in life. My core values helped me navigate these specific endeavors. I am grateful that God has shown me wisdom through marriage, the military, and my growing faith. Keeping God at the core of your being, will ensure that you have a blessed life.

My Prayer:

I thank God, the Father of our Lord Jesus Christ for creating us. My prayer is that we can find peace in the core of our being and turn over our worries to you, our Lord and Savior who is all-knowing and all-loving. When we allow You to be at the core, You will be enough.

Today I challenge you to get on your knees and pray for the desires of your heart. Afterwards write in a journal a love letter to God. Express your needs and hopes knowing that He will guide and protect you.

>*The LORD directs the steps of the godly.*
>*He delights in every detail of their lives.*
>*Psalm 37:23*

-Wisdom from Women-

"He said to her, 'Daughter, your faith has healed you. Go in peace and be freed from your suffering.'"
Mark 5:34

"Elisabeth" – Age 62

I am an African American woman who has been ex-tremely blessed throughout my life. I am the daughter of a now deceased minister and a now deceased musician. Both parents were humble before the Lord and gave me and my three brothers everything they knew to give to their chil-dren. Being the eldest out of the four, I felt that I had been given the most responsibility. Through the grace of God, our dear aunt was also able to give support to me and my broth-ers. Her guidance helped us to fulfill our destinies. When my father passed, she stepped in and made it possible to continue in the church, stay successful in school, develop our musical talent, and thrive at work. She also helped greatly by assisting our mother throughout that difficult time.

Throughout my life, I was given quality spiritual train-ing, musical training and an excellent education. My fa-ther's side of the family was in ministry. My mother's side were musicians. We experienced much from all levels. Each one of us had a well-defined road to travel. All of the siblings are still living except for one brother who passed away in 2009.

In 2012, I was working on my Doctorate. Not only was I working on it but I was also teaching music – fulltime, Minister of music –and performing.

Well...that is when my life changed considerably. I had a massive stroke. For a period of time, I could not walk or talk – let alone sing. The doctors that worked on my behalf were sent by the heavenly Father. Based upon the diagnosis, I should not be here today. The doctors shaved off my hair because I was bleeding inside my head. There were tubes down my throat because I could not breathe. No one expected me to live. I really don't remember everything that happened, but I was told the details later.

During this time, my family put in my retirement papers and secured a place for me in a rehabilitation center. Over the course of my treatment, I had all kinds of therapy. The medical staff was very kind and knowledgeable. I am extremely grateful for my family, friends, doctors, and staff who enabled me to make great strides. After the rehab center, I stayed with one of my brothers and his family because I could not return to my apartment without assistance. My brother and his wife allowed the therapy to continue at their house. I grew stronger – thanks to God. When I visited my neurosurgeon, he was taken aback because I could stand

and walk without a lot of assistance. I still have my walker and my walking cane and I use them periodically. I know what God can do. I could walk and my speech was getting better each and every day.

Well, it's 2016. I am strong and healthy. I am singing again. I am living with someone special who loves me and loves God. If you were to see me now you would be speechless! There are no outward signs of my struggle. I know that God still has plans for me.

"I know the plans I have for you,
declares the Lord, plans to prosper you and not to harm
you, plans to give you hope and a future."
Jeremiah 29:11

All of the training, education and performances I have done are not in vain. I completely trust God to my core. He knows all things. He sees way down the road. I am in his hands completely!

To God be all the glory.
Amen.

-Relationship Recipes-

Gather the family together for soup

Creamy Potato Soup

4 c peeled potatoes, cubed

1 c (3/4 inch) slice celery

1 c coarsely chopped onion

2 c water

2 tsp salt

1 c milk

1 c whipping cream

3 tbsp butter or margarine, melted

1 tbsp dried parsley flakes

½ tsp caraway seeds

⅛ tsp pepper

Combine potatoes, celery, onion, water, and salt in a large Dutch oven. Simmer covered, about 20 minutes or until potatoes are tender. Mash mixture once or twice with a potato masher, leaving some vegetables pieces whole. Stir in remaining ingredients; return to heat and cook, stirring constantly until soup is thoroughly heated. Yield 7 cups.

Shrimp Gumbo

1 (1-1 ¼ lb) soup bone

6 ½ c water

1 tbsp salt

1 bunch green onions

2 c sliced okra

2 tbsp bacon drippings 1 c peeled chopped tomato

1 pod hot pepper

1 large green pepper, chopped

1-2 tsp dried whole thyme

1 bay leaf

1 lb large shrimp, peeled and deveined

Combine soup bone, water, salt in a large sauce pan; bring to a boil. Reduce heat to low and simmer 1 hr. Trim tops from green onion; chop bulbs and top separately and set aside. Sauté onion bulbs and okra in hot bacon drippings 10 min. Add tomato, and sauté about 5 min. Add 6 cups soup stock, green onion tops, and next 5 ingredients. Bring to boil. Cover, reduce heat, and simmer 1 ½ hours. Serve over rice. Yield 2 quarts.

Hamburger Soup

1 ½ lb ground beef

1 medium onion, chopped fine

1 (28 oz) can tomatoes, cut up

2 c water

3 cans consommé or beef broth

1 can tomato soup

4 carrots, chopped fine

1 bay leaf

3 stalks of celery, chopped fine

chopped parsley

½ tsp thyme leaves

8 Tbsp barley

Pepper to taste

Brown meat and onions. Drain well. Combine all ingredients in a large pot. Simmer covered for at least 2 hours (or all day). Serves 10. Freezes well.

Sweet Potato Soup

6 medium sweet potatoes

4 bouillon cubes (dissolved in 8 c water)

10 oz can tomatoes

2 tbsp curry powder

1 c flour

1 c water (cold)

Peel potatoes, dice in large pieces. Bring bouillon cubes and water to a boil, add potatoes, cook until potatoes can be mashed, then add tomatoes. Add curry powder to pot. Blend flour and water in a separate bowl until flour is smooth, then add to potatoes mixture. Cook at full boil for 5 minutes, then simmer 5 minutes. Serve hot. 10-15 servings.

CHAPTER 4

Energy

"I will praise the Lord at all times. I will constantly
speak his praises." Psalm 34:1

God is so amazing. Man was made of dust and God breathed into him to give him life, WOW! It is amazing to think of God's powerful hand in our creation.

Then the LORD God formed a man of dust from the ground,
and breathed into his nostrils the breath of life; and man
became a living being.
Genesis 2:7

This first breath from God gave us the energy to exist. Without the blessing of that first breath we would not be here at all, that was a miracle that is renewed with each inhalation. Every time we breathe, we step into our existence. We become pure energy moving through the world.

Energy is very powerful and so we must take responsibility for the energy we put out into our environment. We must also be aware of the energy we allow into our lives.

I learned about the power of positive energy while in church. I have faithfully attended church ever since I can remember and, to me, going to church was just what you were supposed to do. It wasn't until I was in the 4th grade when something major happened within me that caused an awakening. It's possible that the seed of righteousness leapt into me that day.

I clearly remember looking outside my bedroom window, as I would frequently do, however, this day was different. I started singing spiritual hymns – one in particular was "Do Not Pass Me By."

For some reason I couldn't get this song out of my head. I'm almost certain it was that day when I received the LORD for myself, in my spirit and soul. That week I asked my mother if one of my friends could go to church with us, because her parents weren't attending church at that time. Of course my parents had no problem with her coming. She lived right across the street from us, so that made transportation convenient.

We were so close, like sisters. However, *I* was the big sister. That whole neighborhood was full of "family members." I had brothers, sisters, mothers and fathers all around me. Even to this day, that street still remains a place of love and connection.

Eventually my friend consistently attended church with us on Sunday mornings. Each time we walked into our church home together, I would grin from ear to ear. Having her with me made me feel so good inside, I think it's because it brought us even closer in a different type of way. On some soulful level, I knew she was supposed to be there. She fit right in with us as if she had gone to church with us for years. I remember her joining a few of the children's ministries and she eventually became saved. My church friends became hers and we are all still friends today. I know that was a time when I was used by God to breathe life and divine energy into another person.

"Thus says God the LORD, Who created the heavens and stretched them out, who spread out the earth and its offspring, who gives breath to the people on it and spirit to those who walk in it."
Isaiah 42:5

Can you remember a moment when the Lord used *you* to energize someone? If so, take a moment to reflect on your own experience. Then write down your complete thoughts and feelings.

I wish I could say that I have taken every opportunity to energize others. Unfortunately, that hasn't always been the case. As a matter of fact, there is one time in particular when I really wished I had made an effort to listen to an old friend when all he wanted from me was to talk.

Here is a brief recap of that encounter; I wish the ending had been different:

I was hanging out having dinner with my husband's aunt. As we were about to leave the restaurant a very handsome man walked up to me and stared me in my face with so much intensity that I really wasn't sure if I needed to be flattered or scared.

My fears were quickly calmed, however, when I heard him say my name and, "I can't believe you don't remember me!"

I was perplexed.

"It's me, your first boyfriend from middle school," he said in response to my blank stare. I was suddenly relieved and surprised almost simultaneously. My response to him was "Wow, you have really changed!" But I also started thinking "OMG, this brotha is looking good!"

After a brief conversation, he asked me to call him and said, "I really need to talk to you." I explained to him I was married and I didn't think that it would be good to talk further.

He again insisted I call him, which led me to ask if everything was okay. Instead of answering me directly, he just said, "Rhonda, I want you to call me."

I smiled and said, "No, but it was really good to see you."

As I walked out of the restaurant, a part of me really wished I had gotten his number because I was a little curious and wanted to know what was on his mind.

Not even three weeks later, he committed a crime and then suicide. I was shocked; I couldn't believe this tragedy happened. Immediately my thoughts were: "Could there had been a chance for me to possibly influence, pray or just help my friend to see life differently?" "What would have happened if I had agreed to call him?" I couldn't avoid feeling guilty.

> *"Anyone who is among the living has hope."*
> *Ecclesiastes 9:14*

My friend's death left me feeling empty and depressed. How did I miss this opportunity to offer my energy to this lost soul? Was I being selfish, self-centered, and thoughtless? I was devastated and I didn't know what to do moving forward; I questioned my instincts and judgment.

At some point, I remember calling my sister and crying through my shame. She knew him well, because of our childhood friendship, but she was clueless about why I was crying so much. Through my tears, I managed to tell her about his sudden death, so then she provided comforting words and support.

Despite my best efforts to move on, I kept reliving that one moment. All I could remember was him reaching out to me that night in the restaurant asking for communication. My tunnel vision at the time wouldn't allow me to "hear" him. If only I had been more aware, I could have breathed Christ's love into him at such a critical point in his life.

I eventually went to his funeral, but my heartbreak was so bad I couldn't even take myself to his repast. As weeks went on, I gradually stopped feeling so guilty.

I learned a long time ago that guilt is one of Satan's biggest weapons against us. It is designed to tear us down; it makes us feel dirty, unworthy, and robs of us of our faith and confidence in Christ Jesus. Once I started to pray about my deceased friend, I found relief. As I prayed, I began to feel the spirit of the Lord speaking to me about the dangers of shame. I realized that life is all about living with spiritual victory and having a conscience freed from the guilt of the past.

That was a pivotal moment: I realized that spiritual maturity, along with Scripture and faith, could heal my broken heart. In other words, I decided to reject guilt and shame and, instead, absorb God's love.

> *"You have granted me life and favor,*
> *and Your care has preserved my spirit."*
> *Job 10:12*

Sometimes we allow the strongholds of sin, guilt and other transgressions to linger for months or even years. However, in order to combat this, we must remember God's nature is love, mercy, compassion, kindness and forgiveness. We must breath the energy of God into everyone we meet. It is our calling.

It is also important to recognize the different energy of each person. There is distinct male and female energy that must be acknowledged and understood. I have been married twice, and while this certainly doesn't qualify me as an expert on marriage, I can see how the energy of a husband and wife shows up differently in that sacred relationship.

For wives, this means submit to your husbands as to the Lord. For a husband is the head of his wife as Christ is the head of the church. He is the Savior of his body, the church. As the church submits to Christ, so you wives should submit to your husbands in everything.
For husbands, this means love your wives, just as Christ loved the church. He gave up his life for her to make her holy and clean, washed by the cleansing of God's word.
Ephesians 5:22-26

God's divine plan is crystal clear: man was made head of the home. We women must understand that this doesn't mean he is *better* than us. God created a hierarchy structure within the marital relationship and the family where the Lord placed the role of leadership and accountability upon the man.

"But I suffer not a woman to teach, nor to usurp authority
over the man, but to be in silence.
For Adam was first formed, then Eve."
1 Timothy 2:12-13

There are plenty of women who would consider this a male chauvinistic view, but I think this is God's way of identifying lines of authority.

I have asked God to allow me to marry again. With this request, I have made my intentions known to God and I have humbly asked Him for His best. In my time of waiting, God has told me several things that I must adhere to: first, He assured me to be confident in the silence. I was relieved when I received this message. Then God told me, in life, we all have someone who cares and watches over us. It may be a supervisor, an elder, an official in our city or some other person in a position of authority. In actuality, every man and woman is under the influence of someone else. Now to me, this does not mean those in authority are smarter, wiser, or better than you are. It just means for society to survive, there has to be someone who will assume the role of leader. Within marriage, God ordained that role to the husband as the head of the house and insists he assume that leadership role.

Ladies, we can't forget that Christ is Head of the Church, yet we see Him as He takes the towel and bowl to wash the disciples' feet. Real leadership is humble.

> *"And whosoever will be chief among you,*
> *let him be your servant." Matthew 20:27*

If you are dating and desire to be married, make your request known to God that your future husband understands his role of leadership in the home. Most importantly, his leadership must be with the attitude of Christ and carried out with humility. You must then support him as he assumes this sanctified position within your marriage.

Through my reading of the Bible, I have observed where it tells wives to be submissive. There are also strong statements in the Bible that the husbands must love the wives. In my mind, it is not hard to be submissive to one who deeply loves you. What do you think?

My thoughts are that it is relatively easy to follow someone who leads with selfless love. Therefore, I encourage ladies to understand their role forward and backwards *before* marrying. Since God requires you to be submissive, He will not make this demand hard to endure.

And, please, allow God to bring your future husband to you.

Trust in Christ, always. Marriage is a ministry that will be blessed so you can better serve Him together. When the energy within a marriage is in balance, the relationship is filled with peace, harmony, and prosperity.

My Prayer:

I thank God, the Father of our Lord Jesus Christ for giving us marriage as a ministry. Please guide us in our partnerships so that we can be helpmates to our spouse.

I pray that you can tap into the energy of Christ with every breath you take. Ask for strength and focus as you work through your day. Energize others with your presence and encourage them to tap into their own divine connection with God.

And to those who are married or hope to be married, may your marriage receive the blessings of God.

"The Spirit of God has made me. And the breath of the Almighty gives me life."
Job 33:4

-Wisdom from Women-

Where there is no vision, the people perish:
but he that keepeth the law, happy is he.
Proverbs 29:18

"Joanna"- age 29

"I was raised Catholic. Not a die-hard Catholic, like those who attend religiously and go to confession to be forgiven of their sins for the week. I was one of those Catholics who would only attend Mass on Easter Sunday and Christmas. Those are the only times I remember going to church.

After moving around from time to time my mother settled in Florida. We lived in a very nice community. My new friends were amazing. I met this one girl who became one of my best friends. She invited me to her Pentecostal church. I really enjoyed their worshipping. The music was very different from the choir at the Catholic Church that I was used to hearing. After a while of attending the Pente-costal church, I received the Lord as my personal Lord and Savior for the very first time. I felt a connection that I had never felt before. I was introduced weekly to who God was and how he gave his only son to die for our sins. This built the foundation of the relationship that I currently have with the Lord. Had it not been for my friend, I am not sure how my life would be right now.

Soon after high school I attended college. Things really did not go well for me as I was not focused. I decided to join the military, which in my mind was the best thing for me to do. I had been withdrawing from my classes and failing other classes. The military was so different for me. I was on active duty and now had the freedom to do as I pleased, since my mom kept me so secluded from the world. I dated quite a few guys while in the military. After the completion of my time, I decided to get out of the military and finish school. I was more focused and mature at this time and wanted to get a good career.

I never really had anyone special in my life, still dating guys here and there. By this time all of my high school friends were married and had kids. I felt as though I was the only one with no serious partner. Time was flying by and still no potential husband was on my horizon. I continued to wait patiently, in hopes that I would find someone who would put God first in their life and in our relationship. I got really tired of friends and family asking when I was going to get married knowing I didn't even have a potential partner.

One day I decided to have a talk with the Lord and I told the Lord that I felt I was getting older and that I would not care if I were to marry. I was willing to give my all to the

Lord and I actually felt content and felt peacefulness in my soul.

Then one day, God introduced me to my husband. It was totally unexpected. I had no idea that marriage was waiting for me. I met my husband in Virginia. He is a kind, caring, and the most patient person I have ever met. He spiritually completes me. I tend to have a lot on my plate. I am constantly rushing to get things accomplished and when things get bad and I feel like I can't handle the situation, my husband brings the calm to my storm. We have been married for five years now and I could not have asked for a better partner, someone that I truly want to spend the rest of my life with. We are currently struggling to have kids, however we have both prayed about it and if it's God's will we will conceive and if we can't, I know that God will give us other options to consider. God has been the light in my life. He has kept me from harm in so many ways. Just when I think I have accepted what I think God wants he continues to surprise me with better and greater things. For those who believe that marriage is never going to happen trust and believe that He is working and preparing the right man for his daughters."

-Relationship Recipes-

Collect the family together for lunch

Spinach Casserole

2 pkg chopped spinach drained

1 can cream mushroom soup

2 eggs beaten

1 c mayo

1 c shredded cheddar cheese

Cook and drain spinach. Beat eggs and combine all ingredients. Pour into greased dish and bake at 350 degrees for 45 min.

Shrimp Creole

¼ c butter

1 larger onion, chopped

½ c chopped green pepper

1 clove garlic or garlic powder

½ tsp salt and pepper

1 (8oz) can tomato sauce

1 tsp sugar

1 tbsp Worcestershire sauce

2 tbsp cornstarch

1 lb cooked, cleaned shrimp
1 tbsp old bay seasoning salt
1 tbsp chili powder
Dash of hot sauce

Melt butter in saucepan, Add onion, green pepper, and garlic; sauté 10 min or until tender. Add salt and pepper and tomato sauce. Bring to a boil. Reduce heat, add raw shrimp and remaining ingredients and simmer until shrimp is cooked through and pink. Serve over rice.

Thai Chicken Salad

1 broiler fryer chicken, cooked, skinned
1 cucumber, peeled, seeded, shredded
2 c fresh bean sprouts
2 fresh green chilies, seeded and shredded
½ small red onion, sliced thin, broken into rings
1 tbsp shredded fresh ginger
lime-mint dressing (recipe follows)
½ c chopped fresh cilantro (roots, stems, leaves)
¼ c chopped peanuts

Make lime-mint dressing first and set aside. Cut chicken into thin shreds. In large bowl, mix together chicken and cucumber. In another bowl, mix together bean sprouts, chilies, onion, and ginger. Stir together lime-mint dressing, chicken cucumber mixture. Sprinkle with cilantro and chopped peanuts. Yield: 4-6 servings.

Lime-mint Dressing

¼ c fresh lime juice

3 tbsp fish sauce

2 tbsp vegetable oil

5 tsp sugar

1 tbsp mint leaves

2 garlic cloves, minced

½ tsp salt

Stir until sugar dissolves

White Christmas Punch

1 ⅓ c sugar

⅔ c water

1 c evaporated milk

2 tsp almond extract

2 half-gallons vanilla ice cream, softened

4 (2 liter) bottles lemon-lime carbonated beverage, chilled

Combine sugar and water in sauce pan. Cook over medium heat stirring constantly until sugar dissolves. Remove from heat and add evaporated milk and almond extract. Chill thoroughly. When serving, add ice cream and lemon-lime carbonated beverage. Combine and stir gently. Makes 3 gallons.

CHAPTER 5

Enticing

"Let us walk with decency as, in the daylight; not in carousing and drunkenness; not in sexual impurity and promiscuity; not in quarreling and jealousy."
Romans 13:13

I saw my parents having sex. It's an experience many children have endured since the beginning of time. I wasn't trying to be nosey or disrespectful, but I heard their playful laughter and I wanted to see what they were doing. When you're young you assume that your parents' worlds revolve around you and you can't imagine them having fun without you. To that extent, I had to investigate!

When I saw them with naked limbs entangled, I intuitively knew that I shouldn't be watching. Almost as quickly as I had tiptoed up to their door crack, I raced back to the safety of my childhood bed. I didn't understand what I saw and I wondered how or when it would be explained to me.

Over time I witnessed other elements of sexual intercourse: my father's adult magazines, a couple kissing, seductive scenes in a movie, and racy conversations that were probably foreplay. I didn't know what it all meant, but I had a sense that it was all related. I definitely knew it made me uncomfortable and I wasn't sure how to respond when I encountered it.

My parents loved each other, and they loved me, but they never found a way to bridge the gap that would have allowed me to understand how a healthy, spiritually-aligned sexual relationship develops.

This silence around sex caused me confusion, but also put me in danger. When I was still quite young, around the age of 12, I was very developed for my age. I had large breasts and my cycle started while still in elementary school. Boys took notice of me at school, but I generally ignored them. Men, however, started noticing me as well. My mother never talked to me about puberty or my changing body. I had no frame of reference for what I was feeling on the inside or how I looked on the outside. I definitely didn't know what to do in response to additional male attention

On a trip to the grocery store around this time period, a handsome man approached me and slipped his phone number in my pocket. I hardly knew what was going on, but I heard him say, "Please call me."

I was young and curious, so I dialed his number and talked to him on the phone. I had no idea why he would want a young girl like me to call him. No one had given me any tools to handle this type of situation. Since I didn't discuss these types of matters with my mother or father, it didn't occur to me to talk to them about it.

When he answered the phone, I thought he was nice. He and I talked for a bit and he reminded me of my father. More specifically, he was talking to me in the same way I had seen my father talk to my mother. He waited until my guard was down to make the situation sexual.

First he asked me what I was wearing, then he asked me to lie on my bed and take off my underwear. I questioned him along the way, but he instructed me to do as I was told because he wanted to teach me how to make myself feel good. When he told me to lick my fingers and rub my clitoris, I was completely confused. I didn't even know where that was. Instead of my mother telling me about my body and what to expect in my first sexual encounter, I had a stranger explaining the different parts of my vagina to me over the phone. At some point I decided not to engage with this man anymore and I only pretended to do what he requested. Eventually he climaxed and sighed dramatically. I lied and told him I was pleasuring myself when I was really listening to him and wondering why I was on the phone with this man in the first place.

He encouraged me to call him again, but I never did. I avoided interactions like that in the future. In retrospect, I'm glad that's all the farther it went. Other young ladies are lured into relationships with controlling males or even pedophiles because they don't understand what is happening. This happens when young girls are unaware or misinformed. Worse still, some girls are abducted, raped, or forced into the sex trade. It's so important for us to talk to our children, both girls and boys, about their bodies, appropriate interactions, and keeping their sexuality sacred.

A lot of lessons came from this experience. If Satan can corrupt your mind and steer you away from the simplicity of Christ and His gospel- then he feels like a champion. Also Satan will harass you with some form of fleshly afflictions, but most importantly Satan's goal was to prowl about to seek to capture and destroy me. Now that I have the tools of knowledge to protect myself, I feel it is my duty as a mother, and as a woman, to steer my daughters in the direction of safe, non-sexual interactions with any men they encounter.

This poem/letter speaks to that understanding:

Protect Me Father

Dear God,
Protect me from the people who want me to live their way
Instead of following you.
Protect me from their temptation and help me to walk
The path that is true.

Protect me from the enticing treats that lead to sin
And spiritual pain.
Protect me from the folks who deny your love and
Encourage Earthly gain.
Protect me from the ones who promise ease and
Comfort away from your care.
Protect me from those who hope for my ignorance
So they can catch me unaware.
Each day your protection is all I need
To stay on track and follow your lead.
You are the one who will watch over me
You are the way for all souls to be free.

– Author Unknown

"Keep watching and praying that you may not
come into temptation; the spirit is willing,
but the flesh is weak."
Mark 14:38

We are all called to ask God for protection like the poem describes. When we align ourselves with His guidance, we are better able to avoid enticing situations that can lead to sinful encounters. We must be watchful and guide our children so that they, too, will be safe. Life is full of choices and we must decide if we are going to do things our way or God's way. Like Tyler Perry's movie, "Temptation," we must avoid the traps that lead to heartache and self-destruction. When we choose God's path we are blessed with grace and redemption.

"...but watch out! Be careful never to forget what you yourself have seen. Do not let these memories escape from your mind as long as you live! And be sure to pass them on to your children and grandchildren."
Deuteronomy 4:9

Being enticed doesn't always mean there's a sexual temptation. Sometimes enticement shows up when you know right, but you are allured or attracted into doing something wrong. When we commit a sin, whether because of greed, selfishness, jealousy or just plain old evil-doing, God still allows us to seek healing and forgiveness.

I have knowingly "done wrong" before and here is how I was healed: through putting God's Word to work. The Word of God denotes God's Promises. I remind myself that in James 5:15 it states "And the prayer offered in faith will make the sick person well; the Lord will raise them up. If they have sinned, they will be forgiven. "

God goes on to say that if we confess our sins to each other and pray for each other, we will be healed. We should always remember that the prayer of a righteous person is powerful and effective. I'm sharing this particular

Scripture with you simply because sometimes we do things that may have brought shame to ourselves or love ones, but there is still room for grace. We can still seek forgiveness after discovering that the enticing act wasn't worth the temporary gratification.

Remember: the enemy is truly happy when we stumble– therefore I'm so relieved and happy to know that if I confess my sin I will be forgiven and my pain will be healed.

The awesome God that we serve doesn't end His promise there. He goes on to say in James 5:20 "Whoever turns a sinner from the error of their way will save them from death and cover over a multitude of sins." This is a moment to shout, Hallelujah! It is my desire and my request to God that when you hold your Potluck gatherings, you allow a moment of healing to take place among the participants. This is a perfect time to watch how God will move in a miraculous way in everyone's life.

Remind others that there are so many forms of temptation that lure us into coveting someone or something. These temptations that take us further away from Him are never God's will. There have been so many tragic situations due to excessive use of drugs, alcohol, and money. These variables may appear acceptable initially until they consume our lives and we are no longer in control of them; instead they are controlling us.

I happen to be allergic to alcohol, some laugh, but I feel as though I have been blessed not to be able to consume this substance. I'd like to think this was God's way of protecting me from a potential vice that may have been a stronghold of mine.

There was a time in my life when I can remember witnessing friends doing drugs and consuming alcohol. Tragically, I recall one day when I was in high school when it was announced that a very good friend of mine died during a car accident. She and others were found with drugs and alcohol. Getting high was something she enjoyed doing. I never understood why, but since I wasn't enticed to join in, I never became interested myself.

It saddens my heart when I hear or see reports on the news about teens with drug and/or alcohol addiction. The devil tries very hard to get all our attention away from God. When we feel hurt, alone, or confused, we need to turn to our heavenly Father, not a vice that numbs our pain. If it's not God's will, it's so important to "Just say No."

<u>My Prayer:</u>

I thank God, the Father of our Lord Jesus Christ – I pray that we live as children of light for light illuminates goodness, righteousness, and truth.

I pray that you can reflect on your story around sex, physical temptation, drugs and alcohol. Find peace with your past and ask for God's loving protection as you move forward in your life. Make a commitment to support others who are trying to remain physically pure and whole.

"Let us think of ways to motivate one
another to acts of love and good works."
Hebrews 10:24

-Wisdom from Women-

"Children, obey your parents in the Lord,
for this is the right thing to do."
Ephesians 6:1

"Naomi"- age 38

My mother never held back. She told me everything and anything, but in an age appropriate way. When I asked her about my body parts, versus my bothers', she explained to me how girls and boys are physically different. When I wondered aloud about humping, she explained how that was connected to sex and that a man's body parts could go into a woman's body parts. I learned about reproduction in the process, but my mom addressed the act of sexual intercourse first before adding on additional information.

I always felt safe asking her questions, even ones that now make me wince: "Mom, are you and Daddy going to have sex tonight?"

"Honey, that's not a polite question to ask someone."

"Why?"

"Because it's private and it's not nice to ask someone something that private."

"Oh, okay. Goodnight!"

I left that interaction, not with shame or confusion, but with a level of clarity and understanding that we all hope for as we navigate life while a young person.

My mother respected me enough to patiently discuss whatever issues came up. As a young girl she empowered me to seek information and gave me the tools to process very sensitive concepts. She didn't just tell me about sex, she also gave me a context for how it shows up in conversations, relationships, and family building.

The second step to my in-home sex education was my ability to decide. I could decide to wait until marriage to have sex. No one got to decide that for me. No amount of pressure or temptation could sway me from my path.

Because of my mother's guidance, I felt 100% in control of my body and I was not shy about discussing sex with others. Once I started dating in high school, and later in college, I always told my date that I would not be having sex with them. They invariably laughed at my candor, but I stood my ground with a smile.

"No, I'm not joking. I really like you and I'd like to go out with you, but I need you to understand that I'm waiting until I get married to have sex. I just don't want to lead you on or have a misunderstanding later on."

Around that point they'd stop laughing and I'd let them know I wouldn't be offended if they preferred to ask someone else out on a date. They never did, and they all respected my boundaries. There were no misunderstandings, because we all understood. We, or should I say, I, was clear from the very beginning. No bait and switch, no last minute/heat of the moment decision-making needed.

Being a parent is tough. You have to be so many things for your children. One of the best gifts you can give them is information and context. My mother empowered me to use what I learned to make the decisions that honored my body, aligned with my religion, and respected the men I interacted with. She gave me permission to resist temptation and live my values.

-Relationship Recipes-

Assemble the family together for snack/appetizers

Amy Dip

1 package cream cheese (block), softened
1 jar of medium salsa
1 small bag of shredded cheddar cheese
small can of green chilies and/or sliced black olives
(optional)

Spread cream cheese on the bottom of an oven-safe platter. Pour and spread salsa on top of cream cheese. Sprinkle entire bag of cheese on top of salsa. Sprinkle chilies and/or sliced black olives on cheese, if desired. Bake in a 350-degree oven for 15 minutes or until cheese bubbles. Serve with tortilla chips.

Honey Chicken Wings

2 lbs. chicken wings separated
1 ⅓ tbsp oil
⅓ c soy sauce
⅔ c honey
⅓ garlic clove, finely chopped

2 ½ tbsp ketchup

Salt and pepper

Preheat oven to 375 degrees. Place chicken wings in greased baking dish. Combine all remaining ingredients and pour over wings. Bake 1 hour or until done and sauce is browned. Serve hot or cold.

Zucchini Bread

4 c coarsely shredded zucchini

3 c all-purpose flour

2 ½ c sugar

1 ¼ c vegetable oil

4 eggs, beaten

4 tsp vanilla

2 tsp ground cinnamon

1 ½ tsp salt

1 ½ tsp baking soda

1 tsp ground cloves

½ tsp baking powder

1 c chopped nuts

Heat oven to 325 degrees. Generously grease bottoms only of 2 baking pan 9 x 5 x 3 inches. Beat all ingredients on low speed for 1 min, scraping bowl constantly. Beat on medium speed for 1 min. Pour into pans. Bake until wooden toothpick inserted into center comes out clean, about 1 hr. Cool for 10 mins, remove from pans. Cool completely before slicing.

Spiced Tea

½ lb tea

4 tbsp grated orange peel, dried

2 tbsp grated lemon peel, dried

⅓ c whole cloves

2-4 inch cinnamon sticks crushed

1 tbsp grated nutmeg

1 c (½ lb.) candied orange peel

Mix together and store in glass jar or tea canister. This makes a lot but will keep all winter

CHAPTER 6

Power

"The Sovereign Lord is my strength; he makes my feet of a
deer, he enables me to tread on the heights."
Habakkuk 3:19

So many of us don't know or understand the divine power that lives inside of us. For those who do appreciate our Christian blessings, sometimes we don't demonstrate our joy! Even when there are times of unexpected events or activities that hurt or disappoint us, we have power. Why? If we know that God is with us, how could we be powerless? I admit, at times, I have not acknowledged the power that I have living in me. If I ever start to feel like a victim, I pray that Christ will keep me in a victorious posture and remind me of my strength.

There have been moments throughout my life when I allowed my power to become diminished. At those times I was not as strong as I could have been. I did this only because it was important for me to remain liked or loved. As my life required me to mature because my responsibility began to increase that's when it dawned on me – I can free myself. What does power mean – the ability to do some-thing or act in a particular way?

> *"I can do all things through Christ,*
> *who strengthens me."*
> *Philippians 4:13*

My mother was notorious for exercising her power; in both good or bad situations. This woman wasn't afraid, nor was she willing, to put up with mess. Lord knows I truly admired my mother and I miss her very much.

It was my mother's strength that taught me how to stand up for myself when I was confronted with a middle school bully. It was her power that showed me to always stand up for what is right.

When I reflect back to my middle school days, I remember an unpleasant moment that I had with my art teacher. For some reason I felt like this teacher didn't like me. Don't get me wrong, I didn't care that much for her either. But this particular day I wasn't feeling well and I had asked if I could go to the restroom because my stomach was bothering me.

In a condescending tone, she responded saying "I need to go to the restroom too, because my butt hurts. Do you know why?"

I responded with sarcasm, "Yes, I do. It's because you have hemorrhoids!"

Well you know the class laughed and I'm sure she was embarrassed. She immediately ordered me to report to the principal's office. That's when they contacted my mother. I guess the teacher thought that my mother was going to support her actions towards me. That didn't happen. Being an educator, too, my mother didn't take kindly to the teacher telling me that her butt hurts. She was appalled and asked for a meeting with the principal. I was allowed to sit in the office with my mother and the principal when she accused the teacher of implying that her daughter was a pain in her butt! In that moment, I realized that my mother was wielding her power with diginity and respect. I never had any trouble with that teacher again.

Due to my kind-hearted nature, activating my own power took me a long time to incorporate into my life. I've made many mistakes because I didn't rely on my ability to apply my power consistently and effectively.

My list of mistakes is long: I have allowed people, both male and female, to mistreat me. I have stayed in unhealthy relationships longer than necessary. I have been intimated by others who I admired but tolerated their selfishness towards me. And there have been times where I just allowed people to be people no matter how it may have affected me without holding them accountable.

*"No one will be able to stand up against you all
the days of your life. As I was with Moses,
so I will be with you; I will never leave you
nor forsake you."*
Joshua 1:5

As a mother, I teach my daughters how the power of the living God resides in them. They know that during a moment of despair, uncertainty or wrongful doing created by others, that they should call on the name of Jesus. In that moment of prayer, they will be reminded that He is present and all-knowing. Prayer is yet another way to exercise your power!

*"Whatever you ask in My name, that will I do, so that the
Father may be glorified in the Son. If you ask Me anything in
My name, I will do it."*
John 14:13-14

It took heartbreak and abuse for me to remember God's loving gift of power. He never wavered in His devotion to me even though I had completely walked away from Him. Thanks to my faith, I understand that He formed my soul and set me on my human journey. Because of that, He has also provided an ever-lasting protection over me.

I feel Him the most when I am gifted with divine visions for my future. Like Joseph from the Bible, I have been able to hear and see God's plan for me. Despite this precious ability, there have been many times when I have chosen to ignore the path that is so clearly presented to me.

Why do we do this? Why did *I* do this?

Why do we forsake the God who created us and offers us guidance and support?

The simple answer is that we are afraid.

I didn't understand what my dreams and visions meant. It was scary to "see" myself standing next to my mother's coffin in a church full of people without a single tear in my eye.

Why would God let me "see" such a thing?

A few days after this vision came to me, my mother passed away suddenly. We were all in shock and the funeral was almost a blur. I remember standing at the front of the packed church with my black dress on. I looked at my mother in the coffin, looking exactly as she had in my vision, and I noticed that not one tear came to my eye. I had a sense of peace and knowing that comes with a connection to God. I had seen this all come to pass in advance of this reality. God had allowed me to begin processing this moment before I was abruptly confronted by the hand of death. I was prepared.

I'm still not sure why I didn't cry, but I do know that I had a sense of unity with all things that God created. He has allowed me to "see" things throughout my life that were equally confusing, but also equally powerful.

When I was living through dark times because I abandoned the Lord, He still presented wisdom to me in ways that helped me navigate through my challenges. At one point He "showed" me snakes that surrounded me while I stood in faithful calm. I felt caught in a web and trapped by deceit. All of these feelings came from a place of disconnection from my faith.

Later, when a man that I had dated broke into my house and almost took my life, I was spiritually prepared. I stood in faithful calm as he damaged my physical body. I stood with strength through the attack and praised God for the wisdom to deal with the mental illness of my attacker. I feel that my response, while seemingly passive, was what saved me so that I could live on and be the mother to my daughters.

I encourage everyone to develop an intimate relationship with Jesus; allow Him to show you the answers to your prayers before you even ask for them. He is the truth and the life that we all seek while in human form on this Earth.

<u>My Prayer:</u>

I thank God, the Father of our Lord Jesus Christ- I pray that we all are rooted in love having power, together with all the saints; to understand how wide and long and high and deep is the love of Christ.

I pray that you feel the power God has endowed in your sacred human form. Understand your call and step into your purpose so that every day you can rise up and act as His human champion for all those who need an advocate. Use your power for the good of your brother or sister.

"Jesus answered. I am the way and the
truth and the life.
No one comes to the Father except through me."
John 14:6

-Wisdom from Women-

"For God gave us a spirit not of fear,
but of power and love and self-control."
2 Timothy 1:7

"Tabitha"- age 55

I'm a minister, a former teacher, a retired Army Lieutenant Colonel and about to become an Elder in my church community. My daughter was diagnosed with diabetes at the age of 3 and had learning challenges that we didn't recognize until she was in kindergarten. I have always had to fight for her rights in the classroom setting.

Early on it became clear that her school was not equipped to support her and her medical needs. The school didn't even have a nurse! I fought to have a special program in place for her and to have a nurse available in the building. She was able to fully access all aspects of her education once some basic components were in place.

The school community also benefitted because they now had a nurse on hand to help all children. Furthermore, the program that I helped develop for my daughter ended up being valuable for other students with similar learning hurdles.

It wasn't all smooth sailing; the staff was scared of her diabetes and never wanted her to go on field trips. I later found out that the faculty at the school was even building a file against her so that she could be put out of the school. She was difficult: sometimes when she had a diabetic episode she would wet herself or act out. I appreciated their frustration, but my child deserved to receive an education just like all of the other children.

I had to fight for her all through her schooling and when it came time for college, we all worried that she wouldn't make it through. There were definitely moments during those years of advanced schooling that she almost quit. It was just so hard for so long. I know that she often thought about the sacrifices I made and the supportive community she had when she was feeling low. She stepped into her own power and finished her degree, despite all of the tough times. I'm so proud of her!

I was a teacher for 15 years and I realized I wanted to treat my students with the same love and respect that I had for my own children. I knew that I had them for 90 minutes each period and I could fight for their right to have big dreams. It wasn't easy convincing inner-city kids in Birmingham, AL at an all-Black high school that they had a bright future. So many people had told them there wasn't much for them in this world. I remembered my Scripture and chose to teach with power and love.

Now faith is confidence in what we hope for and
assurance about what we do not see.
Hebrews, 11:1

I always taught my students that there was value in having love and respect for one another. Looking back, I can see I led a lot of students to Christ through my example. There weren't high expectations for my all-Black school students. I had to teach them that they could be someone. I did that by sharing God's love. They gained power through that knowing.

Trust in the Lord with all your heart
And do not lean on your own understanding.
In all your ways acknowledge Him.
And He will make your paths straight.
Proverbs 3:5-6

-Relationship Recipes-

Call the family together for dinner

Honey Mustard Chicken

⅓ c Dijon mustard

⅓ c honey

2 tbsp chopped fresh dill or 1 tbsp dried dill

1 tsp fresh grated orange peel

1 (2 ½ lb.) chicken, quartered

Preheat oven to 400 degrees. Combine mustard and honey in a small bowl. Stir in dill and orange peel. Line a baking sheet with foil. Place chicken, skin side down, on prepared pan. Brush sauce on top of chicken; coat well. Turn all chicken over. Gently pull back skin and brush meat with sauce. Gently pull skin back over sauce. Brush skin with remaining sauce. Bake until juices run clear when thickest portion of meat is pierced with a knife, about 30 min.

Surprise Meat Loaf

¼ c cooking oil

2 ½ c frozen hash brown potatoes, partially thawed

½ c green pepper, finely chopped

¾ c shredded cheddar cheese

1 envelope onion mushroom soup mix

½ c water

1 ½ lb lean ground beef

¾ c soft bread crumbs

1 egg

¼ ketchup

Preheat oven to 350 degrees. In medium skillet, heat oil, add potatoes and green pepper and cook covered for 7 minutes. Cool slightly. Stir in cheese. In medium bowl, combine onion mushroom soup and water. Add ground beef and bread crumbs, egg, ketchup, mix thoroughly. Add cooked potatoes and peppers to the bowl. Mix thoroughly. Pour mixture in a loaf pan. Bake for 1 ½ hours or until meat is well done.

Crab-stuffed Red Snapper

⅓ c minced onion

3 tbsp butter

1 can of crab meat

½ c fresh bread crumbs

¼ c fresh chopped parsley

¼ c heavy cream

¼ tsp thyme

4lb red snapper, dressed for stuffing

1-2 tsp pepper and salt

⅓ c dry white wine, mixed with ⅓ c melted butter
*lemon juice can be substituted for wine
Saute onion in butter until golden. Remove from heat and mix in crab meat, bread crumbs, parsley, heavy cream, and thyme. Sprinkle cavity of fish lightly with salt and pepper. Stuff the fish and skewer edges securely. Place fish in a greased baking pan, pour wine-butter mixture over fish. Bake in 400 degree oven, uncovered for 30-40 minutes until flesh is opaque, basting frequently with wine sauce.

BBQ Shrimp
4 tbsp brown sugar
2 tbsp hot sauce
1 clove garlic finely chopped
4 tbsp olive oil
¼ c dry white wine
Salt and pepper
Raw shrimp

Mix together first six ingredients in a bowl to make the marinade. Peel shrimp (leave tails on), devein and butterfly. Place shrimp on skewers. Add shrimp to marinade, marinate for about 20 min. Place shrimp on a hot grill, about 400 degrees for 2-3 min on each side.

Fresh Apple Slaw

1 (8oz) carton commercial sour cream

3 tbsp lemon juice

1 tbsp sugar

1 tbsp poppy seeds

¾ tsp salt

⅛ tsp pepper

4 c finely shredded cabbage

4 ½ c thin apple wedges

Combine first 6 ingredients. Mix well, combine cabbage and apple; pour sour cream mixture top. Stir well; chill at least 1 hour before serving. Yield 8 servings.

Cucumber and onion in sour cream

½ c commercial sour cream

1 tbsp sugar

1 tbsp vinegar

1 medium cucumber, thinly sliced

2 small onions, thinly sliced

½ tsp salt

Combine all ingredients, tossing gently. Cover and chill 24 hours, stirring occasionally. Yield: 4 servings.

Nanas Rich Macaroni & Cheese

1 (8oz) pkg macaroni

3 tbsp butter or margarine

1 ½ tbsp flour

1 ½ c milk

¼ tsp paprika

1 tsp salt (optional)

2 (8oz) pkg sharp cheddar cheese

1 small pkg shredded cheddar cheese

4 eggs

⅓ c bread crumbs

Cook macaroni as directed on package. Thinly slice enough cheddar cheese to use as a topping, set aside. Cut remaining cheese into cubes. In sauce pan, over low heat, melt 2 tablespoons butter and add flour, salt, alternately add small portions of cheese cubes, then milk, then cheese and so on until all cheese and milk are blended. With each addition, keep the consistency smooth. Place macaroni in 2 qt. baking dish. Add 1 tbsp butter and mix shredded cheese throughout. Add 4 thoroughly beaten eggs, coating all macaroni. Pour cheese mix over macaroni. For topping, place remaining cheese slices on top. Sprinkle bread crumbs and bake at 350 degrees for 30-35 minutes or until brown.

Punch with a Twist

2 pkg Kool-aid any flavor

1 c sugar

1 large can pineapple juice

2 qt water

1 qt pineapple sherbet

1 large bottle of ginger ale

Mix first 4 ingredients. Chill. Add ginger ale and sherbet just before serving. Makes approximately 1 gallon.

CHAPTER 7

Sweetness

"Every good gift and every perfect gift is from above, and comes down from the Father..." James 1:17

Falling in love is wonderful, but hard to orchestrate. When I fell in love with Jesus, it became the sweetest relationship I had ever experienced. I can still remember when I was 27 years old and I re-dedicated my life to Christ. I had spent so many painful years on my own trying to live in the world as an independent young woman. Along the way I learned that, despite my valiant efforts, I had become lost and vulnerable in a world that did not value my soul.

If you don't have a relationship with God already, all you have to do is ask to connect with Him. Having that sort of relationship is the definition of sweetness! You will fall in love with Him on a deeper level throughout your life. There are no limits to the amount of peace and joy you can experience!

Once you are in communion with God, you are able to be a better family member; whether you are acting in the role of sister, daughter, nephew, cousin, or spouse. Having a loving relationship with God makes all the difference.

That being said, the sweetness of life isn't always found in the midst of loving and supportive family members. Sometimes we are challenged to stay focused on God's love despite the earthly drama that surrounds us. Soon after marrying my second husband, Maceo, at 35, some of my relatives pressured me to start a family. They planted negative seeds in my mind regarding the health of our future children if I waited much longer to get pregnant. I began to believe some of the things they told me about having children at my advanced age, and I started to be concerned about how our family would develop.

The situation became more complicated in 2007 when doctors told me that a fibroid was sitting on top of my uterus and wouldn't allow me to conceive. Around the same time, Maceo and I decided to become foster parents to welcome a child into our home without endangering my health. I was hopeful, but after 10 weeks of training we decided that we were not called to this particular type of parenthood. I decided to have an operation to have the fibroid removed. Amazingly, in November 2007, at the age of 38, I was able conceive.

My first blood test showed higher hCG levels than normal which would indicate I was further along or carrying multiples. On November 19th I found out there were three heartbeats. I can still remember how excited my husband and I were to see the first heartbeat, but then the doctor said, "I see another heartbeat." Excitement turned to surprise. Moments later she found a third heartbeat. At this point my husband had to sit down. Despite having six sets of twins in my family, this was still a shocking revelation. We later learned that three eggs were individually fertilized which means fraternal triplets. Each of our girls is her own person and very unique.

On Christmas day, we announced our forthcoming parenthood to our family members. Everyone was overjoyed. We hadn't had any new babies in our family for 30 years.

When we brought them home, they all shared one crib. So small and so happy together!

I was extremely blessed during my pregnancy; my health was good and I received so much support from everyone in my life. Even my job gave me 5 months off after the girls were born. The NICU had trained me how to put them to bed and I followed those orders. Starting in the fourth month, all three girls were sleeping through the night. If you're a new parent, you will appreciate this small miracle! They still go to bed early and sleep at least 8 hours each night. The military taught me structure which has given me the tools to raise these young ladies on my own. I enjoy routine and run a tight household with rules and expectations that my children find comfort in.

Ahhh, it feels so long ago, yet almost like it was yesterday. I had such an overwhelming sweet feeling of love the moment I laid eyes on my daughters for the very first time. Feeling their warm bodies on to my chest while gently holding and touching their tiny hands and feet just made me feel so blessed and happy inside. It was at that moment, that I couldn't contain all the expression of love I was feeling for God, my husband and my daughters within my heart. I still remember my tears of joy when I felt this sense of purpose. God blessed me with motherhood and it has been the sweetest role I've ever had.

This has become abundantly clear to me as I continue to raise my three daughters. The triplets keep me on my toes and challenge and delight me almost simultaneously. I adore each of them and appreciate all the lessons they have taught me as their mother. In this particular role, I have learned the sweetness of patience, living in the moment, and enjoying all of God's creation.

"The Lord will command the blessing upon you in your barns and in all that you put your hand to, and He will bless you in the land which the Lord your God gives you."
Deuteronomy 28:8.

My dream is for my girls to soar in "this land". I ask God to give them joy instead of mourning and praise instead of despair. I know that with His guidance, my girls will be blessed in all things.

I had such a thrilling opportunity when my daughters entered 1st grade. They were given a homework assignment in which the parents had to write a very special note or letter to their child. They didn't get to see our letters until the day the homework was collected; it was fun to surprise each of them with individual love notes. Here are the notes I wrote each of my girls:

Dear Traci (T-byrd),

You are my mini-me! On 2 June 2008 at 2:16pm you entered into this world; along with your two sisters Maci at 2:17pm and Staci at 2:18pm and. That was the happiest moment in my life and that was the day everything changed! There aren't enough meaningful words that can express the way I felt when you arrived. What I can say is it was one of the sweetest moments I've ever known. You were my first and biggest baby, but now you are my smallest child. The Lord continues to reveal all of your contradictions as you get older; you are a leader, but also so gentle and affectionate.

I have so many fond memories with you. The way you place your hands on my face and draw me close to you for a hug and kiss, makes my heart melt. Our mommy and daughter talks at night are so endearing; when I'm trying to get you to go to bed and you are trying to convince me why you don't want to go to sleep. I'll always remember those tiny hands that embraced my hands when we were walking side by side. If only you knew, how you just being you makes me feel so proud, I'm sure you would be amazed, Traci.

Your love of reading and writing inspire me, to personally do more of it for myself. You are so inquisitive; just like your father. I know I tease you about being nosy ("Does your nose hurt from being so nosy, Traci?"), but I'm in awe of your love for learning. You get your discipline and focus from me, so I know that you will continue to be a strong student.

Your calm demeanor has also impressed me through the years. You always manage to stay peaceful, even during stressful events. Do you remember when you fell during ballet class when you were three-years old? I can still recall how my heart stopped when you knocked out your front tooth and bled everywhere. You had an empty gap in your mouth for years before your permanent tooth showed up! I also gained some gray hairs when your grandfather locked you in the car along with the car keys. In both situations, you remained calm while we waited for emergency vehicles to show up. I'm so glad that my worries, like my concerns about your health after your adenoid removal, have all been for naught. You are strong and wise and God is watching over you.

As you get older, I want you to know it's important to respect authority, stay loyal to those who love you, do well in school, and never forget to always put God first in your life. Walk in complete confidence knowing that your dreams will come true when you are faithful to God; even Traci's Tasty Treats, your bakery! T-byrd also remember that your sisters are you sisters, they are not your daughters! Be mindful when you are communicating to the best friends that you will ever have in life. Others may come and go, but your sisters will be by your side no matter what.

It's fun to think about how, at eight-years old, your favorite color is pink, any shade of pink, and your favorite treats are super healthy: water, milk, a sip or two of juice, and green vegetables. You are one of a kind, Traci!

BIG HUGS and a COLOSSAL AMOUNT OF KISSES ALL FOR YOU!

Love,

Mommy Tinkerbell

Dear Maci, (Pumpkin)

When I think of you I'm reminded of how close we are. Our closeness began while you were still in my womb. You are my rib baby! That's how I identified you way back then. While carrying you and your sisters, I didn't experience too many days of discomfort. However, it was pri-

117

marily you that I did feel when activity was going on inside my womb. I remember talking to you the most, because you demanded my attention; just like you do now. Mom! Mom! Mom! You shout my name until I come running or scream WHAT IS IT, Maci! I never get upset, because I remember it was you who gave me such a motherly feeling before I knew your name or even what you looked like. You see, you were positioned on my right side up near my rib cage. From time to time it was uncomfortable, but nothing to fret about, because I loved you and handled you with care. Plus, I understood you were only trying to get my attention for yourself because you needed me to love at you at that particular time. Just like you need special Mommy-May time now.

Maci, although you favor your dad so much in physical traits, your personality is a lot like mine. When I was young like you, I remember I always wanted to become a dentist. I was shocked when you told me years ago that you want to become a dentist when you get older. I just smiled and said, yep you belong to me. Pumpkin, you are the joker in our family. You're always cutting up and laughing when no one else is thinking about laughing. What's wrong with you, I always ask. Of course, jokingly.

The only other thing you take seriously in conversations is talk of becoming a ballerina. I'm always impressed with how you balance your analytical mind with your athleticism; you are a good student and equally talented in dance! I pray that you use your mind for good and not just manipulating Mommy to run errands for you!

I appreciate how you are reserved. Often times it takes you a while to warm up to others. I know that you are cautious about who you trust. That quality within you will serve you well. Life can be tricky, therefore thinking ahead and processing situations thoroughly is an asset. That being said, please don't take too much time when taking a timed exam. The two don't go together! I say this with a smile on my face; your sense of urgency may need to increase sometimes, Pumpkin. You have been gifted with both street-smarts and cleverness. When you learn how to master your time, everything will always work in your favor.

In closing, I know it was because of you that I became a better person, because patience was never my strong suit. I love you for that and so much more! I pray that God bless you with your heart's desires and you bless others with the gifts that God and I have unselfishly given you. You made Star of the Week in school; however, you are always a star to me. Congratulations on your achievement!

While I think it is interesting that you don't have to be in front of others or in the limelight, I see how you can make an impact on everyone around you even when you are in the audience. You and Staci are fashionistas; and I love your sense of style. I can always count on you to pick out your favorite colors: purple and yellow! I also want you to remember how your eight-year old tummy loves chicken and any type of meat as well as sweet tea. I'm not sure why you prefer salty treats to sweet ones, but I do know that you'll always be my sweet Pumpkin!

Love you to the moon and back,

Mommy Tinkerbell

Dear Staci, (CoCo Chanel)

The Lord really blessed me when He gave me you. You have one of the kindest spirits that a person could have; you're like a walking angel. Your affection for me and others is so genuine. You are my miracle baby. Born into the world weighing only 1.4lbs. Now, you outweigh both of your sisters, Traci and Maci. You were determined as an infant to make a lasting impression and I truly believe that everywhere you go, people will always remember you. I'm so proud to have you as my daughter!

The funny thing is you strut with high intensity and an abundance of confidence. No self-esteems issues with you! I love that sense of ownership that you have within yourself. I don't know why I'm surprised, it's a gift that I'm sure I have passed on to you. I'm only kidding. It's what makes you unique. Staci, you aren't afraid to be different.

You have branded yourself, by wearing headbands in your hair with flowers attached to them. This is your own creation. Maybe that's why you have been saying that you want to become a fashion designer. I pray that your dream comes true. There is something else that stands out about you, and that is your relationship with God. You have a special gift. You are able to hear the voice of God and talk about it freely.

I discovered this when you were only three years old. You have always had a special connection with the Holy Spirit. When you were three you woke up in the middle of the night crying. I remember you prophetically telling me, "Mommy, Daddy's not going to come home from the hospital." At that time there was no indications that he wouldn't recover from his illness. Even though he had kidney and liver transplants, we expected him to heal completely. Unfortunately, your insight was accurate and your father, my beloved Maceo, never returned to our home again.

To this day, you surprise me with your intuitive and healing perspective. When you were seven years old, you asked if I was lonely, and I said yes. I admitted that I missed Daddy sometimes. "Well, Daddy is right here," you replied, pointing to the space between us, "and he's happy, Mommy." CoCo Chanel you then told me, "don't be sad, your husband is coming. Until then, do you want to sleep with

Teddy (her teddy bear)?" I was speechless, all I could think to myself was, "Wow! This is deep."

I'm so grateful to God, just knowing how near He is to our family. It's an awesome feeling! CoCo Chanel, your love for the stories of the Bible have been a part of you for a very long time. You love the story of Joseph (the dreamer). Joseph is definitely your favorite leader from the Old Testament. I'm sure as you grow, you will learn more about the other men and women from the Bible.

Your current interests keep me very busy: you are a member of the chess club, you are a gymnast, you take sewing lessons, and you continue to make the honor roll just like your sisters. I'm glad that God has provided me the resources to be able to expose you and your sisters to these opportunities. Somedays it wears me OUT, but I wouldn't have it any other way. I love you.

Now, orange, green, and yellow are your favorite colors. And one day you say you're going to live in Paris, France. Don't forget to send me a ticket! I've never been to France. When you get there let the cooks know that when it comes to meals, you could live on lemonade and pasta. As your mother, I'm advising you to eat your vegetables!

Love always and forever,

Mommy Tinkerbell

My Prayer for my Daughters:

Dear God

I kneel and bow in honor of You thanking You for my bundles of joy. I'm truly grateful to have been blessed with my daughters, Traci, Maci and Staci. The unconditional love that pours from their heart to mine, sometimes leaves me speechless. This special gift of motherhood is never taken for granted. Having birthed three children at one time is amazing. God, thank you. You knew I would have been alone after the death of Maceo, therefore, You equipped me with more than I could ask for.

In Ecclesiastes 4:12 "A person standing alone can be attacked and defeated, but two can stand back-to-back and conquer. Three are even better, for a triple-braided cord is not easily broken." I pray for their lives to be enriched with faith and that each one of them will be mighty in this land as You have promised. My hope and belief for them is for Your anointed strength, courage and wisdom to overcome any obstacle that should come their way.

Also, I pray that their dreams line up with Your will and their seeds will harvest an abundance of fruit. This fruit will last from generation to generation, so that the stream of greatness will be upon our family forever.

In Jesus' name,
Amen

My Prayer:

I thank God, the Father of our Lord Jesus Christ – I pray that each of us have the Spirit of love, joy, peace, patience, kindness, goodness, faithfulness, gentleness and self-control as long as we live.

"May the Lord, the God of your ancestors, increase you a thousand times and bless you as he promised."
Deuteronomy 1: 11

-Wisdom from Women-

"And we are witnesses to these things,
and so is the Holy Spirit,
whom God has given to those
who obey him."
Acts 5:32

"Sarah" – age 57

I've been on my own since I was sixteen years old. I wasn't from a bad home, just a home of a single mother who had four children and was struggling to do the best she could to take care of us. At the time I didn't understand her struggle, but as I grew older and had children of my own and raised one of them by myself I can understand and empathize with what she was going through. Her choices may not have always been the right or the best choices, but they were her choices and I can honestly say at this point in my life.... I respect her for the sacrifices that she had to make for us.

Throughout my life, I have had struggles. I joined the military, got married and had a baby at a very young age and I believe because I was so young the marriage did not last. We divorced within the first two years. The years that followed would bring a lot of dates, dinners, and I'm sad to say a few one night stands. Thirteen years after the first marriage "I" picked another man and decided to marry him. We were good together for a while, but being young and naive, I learned the hard way that there should be more to a relationship that just sex.

After my second marriage failed, I started out doing the same things I had been doing, dating here and there and trying to be in relationships with the wrong people. It took another five long years for me to realize that I did not HAVE to be in a relationship, that I could be fine all by myself. It was after this realization that I started to just live for me and my daughter alone. I bought a house and two vehicles. I put my five-year plan down on paper so I could visualize it and I began to set it into motion.

GOD said, "Now she is ready". He put a person in my path who had already been there for almost two years. Because I wasn't ready, GOD didn't allow me to see him before that time. Once I was ready, he removed the blinders from my eyes and all the hardness and hurt from my heart and HE allowed me to receive the gift that he was giving me.

Our first date was on Valentine's Day, which is supposed to be the day for love. Well for me it was the day I fell in love. We met for drinks and talked for a while, then we went to meet some of his friends for dinner. The evening was going so well that we decided to join them at another spot to listen to a band, but we ended up sitting in a booth talking the entire time. We had such a connection and so much in common, it was unbelievable.

After the show was over we decided to go for a drive and ended up parked by the water and talked until the sun came up. I had NEVER had a connection like that with anyone in my entire life. After we went home and got a few hours of sleep, we talked and spent the entire weekend just hanging out. It was magical!! Over the next few weeks we were inseparable. Less than two months into this whirlwind relationship, we went to a function in D.C. with some friends and we had a wonderful time. When the event was over we were coming up the stairs and he began to shout over and over, "I love this woman". I thought, "Oh Lord, he has had too much to drink".

Let me pause for a moment and say that I have been in church my entire life, but I would never describe myself as spiritual. I had never been overcome by the Spirit or shouted.

Now, as we were coming up the stairs, I put my arms around him in an attempt to calm him down, but what I got was a jolt that went through my body. Before I knew it my body jerked backwards and I dropped my purse and kicked off my shoes and began to shout, right there on that sidewalk in D.C. at around three in the morning.

My friends, who were also from my church, placed a prayer circle around me and let me go. What I did not know was that He was shouting also and they had a prayer circle around him. I think this went on for about an hour. We shouted, we prayed, we had church! Right there on that sidewalk!!

We were married two months later and have been married now for twelve wonderful years. We have a beautiful 11-year-old daughter and we could not be happier. There were a few bumps and bruises during our adjustment period, but we are truly happy now and looking forward to raising our daughter and growing old together. We have adopted a motto that gets us through any and everything. "GOD'S GOT THIS."

-Relationship Recipes-

Keep the family together for dessert

Baked Apples

6 large baking apples

6 tsp sugar

1 c chopped walnuts

1 c raisins

1 graham crackers or 5 vanilla wafers

1 tbsp of butter

½ tsp cinnamon

Fresh lemon with grated rind

Wash and slice off top and core apples. Preheat oven to 350 degrees. Mix butter, nuts, raisins, cinnamon, grated lemon rind and crushed graham cracker and sugar in bowl. Wrap lower half of apple with foil. Put in baking dish. Fill apples with above mixture. Squeeze lemon juice over filled mixture. Add 1 tsp of water to each apple. Sprinkle with extra cinnamon over apples for taste and color. Bake for 40 to 60 min or until tender but not mushy. Serve hot or cold. Serves 6.

Cheesecake Supreme

¾ c all-purpose flour

3 tbsp sugar

¾ tsp grated lemon peel

6 tbsp butter

1 egg yolk slightly beaten

½ tsp vanilla

3 (8 oz) pkg cream cheese

1 c sugar

2 tbsp all-purpose flour

2 eggs 1 egg yolk

¼ c milk

1 c halved fresh strawberries

Strawberry Glaze (recipe below)

To prepare crust, combine ¾ cup flour, 3 tbsp sugar, ½ tsp lemon peel. Cut in butter crumbly. Stir in 1 slightly beaten egg yolk and ¼ teaspoon vanilla. Pat ⅓ of dough onto bottom of 8-inch spring form pan (sides removed). Bake in 400-degree oven for 7 min or until golden; cool. Butter sides of pan; attach to bottom. Pat remaining dough onto sides of pan to a height of 1 ¾ inches.

To prepare filling, let cream cheese soften to room temp. Beat until creamy; add remaining lemon peel and remaining vanilla. Mix 1 c sugar, 2 tbsp flour, ¼ tsp salt; gradually blend into cheese. Add 2 eggs and 1 egg yolk all at once; beat just until blended. Stir in milk. Turn into crust lined pan, Bake in 450-degree oven for 10 min. Reduce heat to 300 degrees, bake 55 min more or until center appears set. Remove from oven; cool 15 mins. Loosen sides of cheesecake from pan with spatula. Cool 2 ½ hr. more; remove sides of pan. Cool 2 hrs. longer.

Place halved fresh strawberries on cooled cheesecake. Pour strawberry glaze over strawberries. Chill at least 2 hrs. Make 12 servings.

Strawberry Glaze

¾ c fresh strawberries

½ c water

⅓ c sugar

4 tsp cornstarch

Crush strawberries, add water. Cook 2 min; sieve. In saucepan, combine ⅓ c sugar and 4 tsp cornstarch; gradually stir in sieved berry mixture. Bring to boil; stir constantly. Cook and stir thickened and clear. Cool to room temp. *May use 1 can strawberry, cherry, or blueberry pie filling instead of homemade strawberry glaze.

Red Velvet Cake

2 ½ c sifted cake flour

½ tsp salt

3 tbsp cocoa

2 sticks of butter (room temp)

1 ½ c sugar

½ c eggs

2 oz red food coloring

1 tsp vanilla

1 c buttermilk

1 tbsp white vinegar

1 tsp baking soda

Sift flour, salt, and cocoa together. Set aside. Cream butter and sugar together. Add eggs to butter and sugar mixture. Blend well and add food coloring and vanilla. Mix buttermilk, vinegar, and soda; add alternately with dry ingredients to creamed mixture. Mix at low speed on electric mixer. Pour batter into well-greased Bundt pan. Bake in preheated oven on 350 degrees for about 30 min or until done.

Million Dollar Pie

1 can sweetened condensed milk

⅓ c lemon juice

⅓ c crushed/drained pineapple
⅓ c chopped cherries
⅓ c chopped pecans
9 oz whipped cream
1 baked pie shell

Whisk milk and lemon juice, pineapple, cherries, and nuts. Fold in whipped cream Pour into baked pie shell and chill. Just before serving, top with additional whipped cream and sprinkle with additional nuts (if desired).

Afterword

God has called you to step into your sacred purpose. You can try to do this on your own, but that was never God's intention. His Son understood the power of connection and the joy of fellowship. Jesus walked on the Earth in constant communion with others. Furthermore, he chose to share his purpose with everyone he encountered. During his short 33 years among us, He engaged with all walks of people and provided love and encouragement to each of them.

It is that call for communion and engagement that brings us together in our churches across the globe. My hope has always been that we can take opportunities to interact with one another in the name of God's love whenever possible. I wrote this book because I wanted to propose a format for fellowship that stretches us to relate through stories and Scripture. I want the stories I've shared here to inspire you to share *your* stories with others. I pray that the meal suggestions within these pages will encourage you to share *your* favorite recipes with new friends. Finally, I hope that the true stories you've read will move you ask others about their experiences. We learn through listening, and, ultimately, this proposal is a call to listen and learn from one another.

They worshipped together at the Temple each day,
met in homes for the Lord's Supper,
and shared their meals with great joy and generosity."
Acts 2:46

Will you accept this mission in your life? If you are ready, I have created a template or blueprint for your own fellowship. Simply fill in the areas listed on the next few pages and then plan a time to share with others in your community. If you want this process to be a group endeavor, encourage others to buy this book and complete their template as well.

Once you all come together with your individual Scripture verses, your reflections, themes, a related story from your life or from someone you know, a "prayer for others," and finally a dish that you prepared (with recipe), you will get to connect with friends, family, or church members on a whole new level.

My prayer will always be that you can grow in your love of God through fellowship, food, and Scripture!

~Lady Rhonda

Recipe of Life

Begin with a cup of salvation
Mix with a pint of grace
Spread with the love of Jesus
Into every available place.

Knead prayer into the mixture
Add fruit from the tree of life
Leaven with patience and kindness
Omit all worry and strife

Flavor with true compassion
Let the milk and honey flow
Sprinkle with joy and gladness
Bake inside the heart real slow

Mix water from the rock of ages
With the blood of Calvary
Then you will always have
Life's greatest recipe.

Christian Best and Kenya Gorham

Acknowledgments

I want to express my deepest, heartfelt thanks to the women who donated their Potluck stories and recipes unselfishly. I pray that your experiences not only bring your love for God closer, but for God to use you to give that kind, supporting spirit to those who lean on you for growth and understanding of God's faithfulness.

Special thanks goes to Keira Jones, Karen Alara and Tammy Brooks, my friends, for hearing the voice of God and being obedient to His will. You all contacted me to validate and confirm what God was waiting so patiently for me to do; write the book! To my Big "lil" sister Sandra Beavers for being by my side from the first day we met. You are always giving me encouraging words and allowing me to be me without judgement. To Catherine Proctor and Keyonna Lacy, for having hearts that love my daughters as your very own grand-daughters and nieces. I know that you two have been called by God to fill a position so my daughters won't ever feel left out.

Special thanks and gratitude to Apostle Angeloyd Fenrick, for teaching me how to study the Bible and Pastor Diane Hugger for spiritual guidance through one of the most challenging seasons in my life. Minster, counselor and friend, Trina Goffe for helping me to process through life triumphs and trials by doing things God's way.

I give honor to God, whom honor is due. As a woman, mother, leader, daughter, sister and friend I have listened to countless stories of joy, sorrow, victory, and disappointment that have allowed me to have a heart full of care and humility towards others. I am extremely grateful for the trust and connection that women of various ethnic groups and ages have extended to me. I'm so appreciative that you have found comfort in expressing your life-changing moments with the readers of this book.

I am so thankful for the editorial contributions of VoicePenPurpose Publishing.

I can't thank the goodness of the Lord enough for continuously blessing me immeasurably. Thank you, Jesus and Hallelujah for always coming to my rescue! It was on 31 December 2011 when God came to me on one weary night and spoke boldly to my inner spirit – He reminded me of how He has already blessed me; He went on to say that when I put all my trust in Him, that He was going to bless me more than what my eyes can see and further than I can imagine. He has kept His promise and I'm extremely grateful that He is pleased with me.

And last, but far from least, thanks to my happy, funny, and loving daughters: Traci, Maci and Staci, who are my sources of daily inspiration as well as the love that lives in my heart for my dad, Ronald Chase, my sisters: Rachelle, Rolawnda, and Roshawnda, and my beloved Aunt Margaret.

"Now all glory to God, who is able,
through his mighty power at work within us,
to accomplish infinitely more than
we might ask or think."
Ephesians 3:20

YOUR Potluck Proposal

Bible Scripture:

Your reflections on this Scripture; how it has impacted your views, and how it shows up in your life:

What theme do you notice from your life/ Scripture?

A Related Story from Your Life or Someone Else's Life:

Your Prayer for Others:

Dishes and songs you'd love to make/play:

About the Author

L ady Rhonda aims to carry out God's will. Her divine calling is to share biblical stories and scriptures while dining amongst women of diverse backgrounds throughout the world.

Lady Rhonda is also a Lieutenant Colonel in the Army National Guard. Proudly, she has 25 years of military service and still going Army strong. Currently, she holds the position of Director, J1-Manpower and Personnel for the

District of Columbia National Guard in Washington, DC.

She has the impressive ability to uphold a demanding professional career, independently raise triplets, and continue to reach for greater achievements, all because she has placed no ceiling or walls on where her future lies.

Lady Rhonda's relationship and faith in the Lord our God is how she is able to maintain strength and peace daily. Lady Rhonda also the President of the Capital Guardian Toast Masters Club (Toastmasters International, District 27) in Washington, DC and is open to expanding her speaking engagements. She is also a VIP member of the Association for Professional Women, a member of the National Guard Association, a member of the District of Columbia Army National Guard, and a member of the Female Officer Making a Change (FOMAC) club. Most importantly, she is a member of the First Baptist Church of Glenarden in Upper Marlboro, Maryland since 2004.

She currently resides in Clinton, Maryland with her three adorable daughters.

Music to listen to while cooking, entertaining, or relaxing:

**Let the word of Christ dwell in you richly,
teaching and admonishing one another in all wisdom,
singing psalms and hymns and spiritual songs,
with thankfulness in your hearts to God.
Colossians 3:16**

"Pray for Me" by Kirk Franklin
"Because You Love Me" by Celine Dion
"I'm Yours" by Jason Mraz
"Worth" by Anthony Brown
"I Hope You Dance" by Lee Ann Womack
"Through The Years" by Kenny Rogers
"Halo" by Beyoncé
"I Love the Lord" by Whitney Houston
"From This Moment On" by Shania Twain
"God Favored Me" by Hezekiah Walker
"Because of You" by Tamia
"A Song for Mama" by Boyz II Men
"Step Aside" by Yolanda Adams
"Great is our Faithfulness" by SE Samonte
"My God Is So High" by Kathleen Battle
"I Found Love" by Bebe Winans

"I Love Him Like I Do" by Deritrick Haddon

"I Luh God" by Erica Campbell

"Intentional" by Travis Greene

"The Way You Love Me" by Anthony Evans

"It's a Beautiful Day" by Jamie Grace

"Overcomer" by Mandisa

"Surrender" by Flame ft. V. Rose

"I Can Only Imagine" by MercyMe

"Nobody Greater" by VaShawn Mitchell

"Next to Me" by Emeli Sande›

"Clean This House" by Isaac Carree

"I need You" by Ty Tribbett & G.A.

"Lucky" by Jason Mraz

"Fill Me Up" by Tasha Cobbs

"Stand" by Donnie McClurkin

"He Still Loves Me" by Beyonce feature Walter Williams

"Strong Enough" by J Moss

For more information about how you can introduce
The Potluck Blueprint in your church community,
please reach out to Lady Rhonda at
LadyRhonda3@gmail.com,
LadyRhonda.com or visit her FB group:
The Potluck Blueprint Collective.

Made in the USA
Middletown, DE
13 December 2016